THE DRAGON'S EMBRACE

BY THE SAME AUTHOR

An African Student in China

EMMANUEL JOHN HEVI

The Dragon's Embrace

The Chinese Communists and Africa

FREDERICK A. PRAEGER, *Publishers*

NEW YORK · WASHINGTON · LONDON

DT
38.9
C5
H4

Frederick A. Praeger, Publishers
111 Fourth Avenue, New York, N.Y. 10003, U.S.A.
77–79 Charlotte Street, London, W.1, England
Published in the United States of America in 1967 by
Frederick A. Praeger, Inc., Publishers

© 1966 Emmanuel John Hevi

All rights reserved

Library of Congress Catalog Card Number: 66–12983

53024

Printed in the United States of America

CONTENTS

THE DRAGON'S EMBRACE

Preface

I believe in non-alignment, but not in the kind that turns men and nations into cowards unable either to defend the principles and ideals they hold or to condemn with deserving vehemence any international injustice and chicanery that affects them directly or indirectly. As for 'aligned non-alignment': I have total contempt for it and for those who practise it.

In Africa for some time now, non-alignment has meant unreasoned opposition to almost everything British, French, American or generally Western. While I admit the need to administer a resounding kick to the Western powers now and then, just to remind them that the old days are gone, I deeply deplore the general African attitude which assumes that imperialism is exclusively the vice of certain nations and political systems. Why, right on the home-front in the continent of Africa, we see the ludicrous spectacle of men trying to grow imperialist on borrowed money. We have had an Nkrumah, now politically dead but not yet buried, for whom no method was foul enough if it promised to unite the whole of Africa under himself.

It should have been clear to us long ago that men and nations that have most recently broken the shackles of imperialism are not necessarily innocent of imperialist propensities. Among the new nations, one can easily cite—beside the examples citable in Africa—the China of Mao, the Cuba of Castro, the now repentant (we hope) Indonesia of Sukarno, and the North Vietnam of

Ho Chi Minh. Since the imperialism of these new nations can affect us as profoundly as, and sometimes even more profoundly than, the same vice in the traditional imperialists, it will pay us to study, with all the care we can give to the subject, the political mentality and attitude of these new and unfamiliar imperialist nations.

Much as we dislike the idea, Africa at the present time is being buffeted by a variety of cold-war cross-currents. Since much of the money to build the schools our children attend, to construct the roads and bridges over which we travel, to raise the big dams that produce electricity to work our factories and water to irrigate our fields, now comes from these same cold-war camps, it is evident that Africa will have to swim in these uncomfortably cold currents for some time yet. The best thing we can do is to try to learn how these currents flow. That should be an important step towards reaching the shores of economic self-sufficiency and political stability.

Some confusion of terminology in a study of this kind is hard to avoid, due mainly to the fact that the terms in question —communism, socialism, capitalism—are very confused in their modern usage. Communism, also known as scientific socialism, meant originally the political system which, theoretically, would guarantee complete security to the citizen, affording him the material necessities of life and ensuring that he contributes to the commonweal. In practice, it has meant limiting his freedom of opinion and action within the stifling bounds demarcated by an omnipotent party. The Marxist version of socialism is the road leading to communism. But the clarity of the terms 'Marxist', 'communist' and 'socialist' has been considerably diluted even by the communist countries themselves, who call themselves indiscriminately 'communist' and 'socialist'. African communists, in a further essay in confusion, call themselves 'scientific socialists' (or, until their messiah fell, 'Nkrumahists') mainly because, as a result of Western colonial tuition, communism as a term is regarded in Africa as thoroughly disreputable.

Capitalism, as defined by Karl Marx, has almost ceased to exist in its traditional homelands. In place of the absolute owner-employer of Marx's day, they now have vast companies and corporations in which the lowliest citizen with his small savings may own a vote-bearing share. The inhuman exploitation, which moved Marx and others to justified revolt against the capitalist system, has largely disappeared. The 'exploited' employee may now have a car or scooter and many quite luxurious domestic conveniences besides. Through powerful unions, he negotiates with his employer how many hours he wants to work in a week, how much pay he wants for his labour, how he wishes to be provided for in sickness and retirement, and so on. With governments and trade unions on the sharp look-out for infringements of workers' rights and privileges, Karl Marx's notion of capitalist exploitation calls for sharp revision.

To skirt the ambiguities in terminology as much as possible and to avoid the derogatory meaning often attached to the words 'communist' and 'capitalist', I have, wherever convenient, used the term 'West' to mean the traditional capitalist countries, whose governments now pass sweeping welfare laws that must be the envy of many communists; and the term 'East' to mean the communist countries, some of whose governments now indulge such traditionally capitalist notions as 'profit motive' and 'decentralisation'.

�◙　　　　　◙

Africa figures prominently in the scheme of Chinese political designs. Unless the protests against China's subversion that have come from the governments of Kenya, Rwanda, Burundi, Cameroon, Ghana, Ivory Coast and many other African states, are to be irrationally dismissed as cold-war propaganda, China's aims in Africa merit more attention than we have so far accorded them. It is with this end in view that I have written this book.

I do not pretend to assume that eighteen months' stay in China makes me an authoritative interpreter of the Chinese mentality and of Peking's African policy. Even so, the experiences I described in *An African Student in China* have left on my mind a deep impression that makes me more interested in Chinese affairs than are many of my fellow Africans. It is to them that this book is chiefly addressed.

Few subjects are as complicated as China's African policy and the motives behind it. I am therefore taking the limited scope of seeking to show that China's intentions in Africa cannot possibly be in the best interests of us Africans. For this purpose, I have found it convenient to use as kingpin of this book the 'Five Principles of Peaceful Coexistence': the main offering to us of Premier Chou En-lai during his African tour, which lasted from December 14, 1963 to February 4, 1964. I seek to show how these Five Principles, and many another of China's noble-seeming declarations, are daily being violated by China in this continent and in other parts of the world.

If this book can, in however small a measure, succeed in showing the way in which at least one of the world's cold-war currents is flowing, my purpose will have been achieved.

Accra, Ghana   EMMANUEL JOHN HEVI
Autumn 1966

ONE

The 'Five Principles' and Chinese Practice

The Chinese communist leaders appear to make no secret of their plans and intentions. They announce just what they are going to do and they list all the points neatly, numbering them methodically. All the campaigns launched on their domestic front follow such a pattern. The 'Three-Antis' was one of the early campaigns which was supposed to attack three common evils of bureaucracy (I do not remember exactly which evils). The result was the disappearance of old 'reactionary' civil service personnel. A campaign of long standing among Chinese army recruits is called the 'Five Good'. Each soldier is supposed to cultivate five specific good qualities, and the 'Five Good' movement also applies to groups at different levels of command. The result, I would guess (I must only guess for I have fortunately avoided any contact with the Chinese army), is that Chinese soldiers and their army commands are much like any others.

I introduce this subject in order to explain that the Chinese communists have a great predilection for neatly numbered policies. It is my opinion, having spent eighteen months in

China, that one should not attach too much importance to these enunciated policies. Remember, for instance, that once 'a hundred flowers' were invited to bloom in a sudden flowering of free speech. But when the first bud began to open, it was promptly trampled under the heavy foot of the Chinese Communist Party gardener.

Communist China's foreign policy is based on the 'Five Principles of Peaceful Coexistence'. These principles first appeared in the preamble to an 'Agreement between the People's Republic of China and the Republic of India on Trade and Intercourse between the Tibet Region of China and India'.* The first part of this preamble reads:

> The Central People's Government of the People's Republic of China and the Government of the Republic of India . . . have resolved to enter into the present agreement based on the following principles:
> 1. Mutual respect for each other's territorial integrity and sovereignty;
> 2. Mutual non-aggression;
> 3. Mutual non-interference in each other's internal affairs;
> 4. Equality and mutual benefit;
> 5. Peaceful coexistence.

It is not quite clear to me why an agreement on trade and the free movement of pilgrims should begin with such broad principles on human and international relations; but I shouldn't be surprised to learn that India (who called the above principles the 'Panch Shila') was glad to have them incorporated in the agreement and may in fact have pressed for their inclusion. China's earlier recolonisation of Tibet, and her reluctance to disavow maps which showed border claims against India and

* Some commentators think that, by giving recognition to the 'Tibet Region of China' in this agreement, India in fact signed away Tibet's freedom, besides revealing herself to China as a weakling.

the Himalayan states, had aroused very natural fears and misgivings in India. Thus the Five Principles, if faithfully adhered to, could have reassured India and ensured peace in that part of Asia. There is little doubt, in any case, that the Indian leaders accepted the principles in good faith and had every intention of observing them. There is equally little doubt that the Chinese leaders attached no more importance to the Five Principles than they did to any of their other neat lists.

This 1954 statement of the Five Principles lulled Indian fears and prepared the way for the 1955 Bandung Conference where Premier Chou En-lai and Prime Minister Nehru met with leaders of Asian and African countries to form the first loose association of Afro-Asian countries. Chou En-lai, who is now considered to have dominated the Bandung Conference to a large extent, actually owed his presence there to Prime Minister Nehru. Having thus opened the door to the Afro-Asian community, using the key of the Five Principles (which had reassured Nehru of China's friendly attitude), Chou proceeded to endorse another virtuous list of 'Bandung Principles'. The new list was similar to the Five Principles but contained, in addition, specific assurances of 'racial equality and non-discrimination' and also 'respect for the freedom to choose a political and economic system'. These added principles, we can now see, underpinned China's bid for participation in, and dominance of, the 'coloured' part of the world, while at the same time reassuring the Afro-Asian leaders that communism would not be pushed down their throats. (Not yet, at least!)

Before we examine how China observes her 'principles', we must add the specific lists for Africa. Chou En-lai's 'Five Principles for Africa' were enunciated in the Sudan in January 1964, during the Chinese leader's extensive African tour. This is the reason why 'Arab' comes before 'African' in the wording. Later, when the list was published in the *Peking Review* (No. 7, 1964), the references to 'Arab' were deleted. The following list is the joint communiqué version:

1. China supports the Arab and African peoples in their struggle to oppose imperialism and old and new colonialism and to win and safeguard national independence.

2. China supports the governments of Arab and African countries in pursuing a policy of peace, neutrality and non-alignment.

3. China supports the Arab and African peoples in their desire to achieve unity and solidarity in the manner of their own choice.

4. China supports the Arab and African countries in their efforts to settle their disputes through peaceful consultation.

5. China holds that the sovereignty of Arab and African countries should be respected by all other countries, and that encroachment and interference from any quarter should be opposed.

At another of Chou En-lai's stops in the African tour—my native Ghana—he spoke out forcefully against Western trade and aid, and then proceeded to announce 'Eight Principles' that allegedly guide China's policy in providing economic and technical assistance to other countries. Here they are, in their full beauty:

In providing economic aid to other countries [Chou's statement runs], the Chinese Government has always strictly abided by the following eight principles:

One: The Chinese Government always bases itself on the principle of equality and mutual benefit in providing aid to other countries. It never regards such aid as a kind of unilateral alms but as something mutual and helpful to economic co-operation.

Two: In providing aid to other countries, the Chinese Government strictly respects the sovereignty and independence of the recipient countries, and never attaches any conditions or asks for any privileges.

Three: China provides economic aid in the form of interest-free or low-interest loans and extends the time limit for the repayment when necessary so as to lighten, as far as possible, the burden on the recipient countries.

Four: In providing aid to other countries, the purpose of the Chinese Government is not to make the recipient countries dependent on China but to help them embark step by step on the road of self-reliance and independent economic development.

Five: The Chinese Government tries its best to help the recipient countries build projects which require less investment while yielding quicker results so that the recipient goverments may increase their income and accumulate capital.

Six: The Chinese Government provides the best quality equipment and material of its own manufacture at international market prices. If the equipment and material provided by the Chinese Government are not up to an agreed specification and quality, the Chinese Government undertakes to replace them.

Seven: In giving any particular technical assistance, the Chinese Government will see to it that the personnel of the recipient country fully master such techniques.

Eight: The experts and technical personnel dispatched by China to help in construction in the recipient countries will have the same standard of living as the experts and technical personnel of the recipient country. The Chinese experts and technical personnel are not allowed to make any special demand or enjoy any special amenities.

Now, what do all these declarations of principle prove—except that the Chinese leaders can count? Obviously, we should accord our highest admiration and deepest gratitude to any country that holds such lofty principles in its relations with Africa. But to hold and faithfully observe one single principle is far more meritorious than to hold a thousand and observe none.

For the 'observing' side of the coin, we might first examine the fate of the Five Principles of Peaceful Coexistence, because the specific principles for Africa are an outgrowth of the earlier ones. In a short preamble to the Eight Principles, Chou claimed —on February 3, 1964, at Mogadishu in Somalia—that, in her relations with the African countries, China has 'consistently and unswervingly' taken her stand 'in accordance with the Five Principles of Peaceful Coexistence and the Ten Principles of the Bandung Conference'. An editorial in the *People's Daily* three days later drove home the argument: 'Premier Chou En-lai and President Nkrumah of Ghana have jointly set forth the five basic principles of international life. *All these principles embody the general line of China's foreign policy.*' (My italics.)

For an understanding of how the Five Principles of Peaceful Coexistence have been observed by Communist China, we need to study her conduct towards her near neighbours. This requires a 'background-glance' at Chinese history.

If the Chinese communists pursue expansionist policies, as they do, it is not just because they are communists. They have, certainly, a messianic urge to spread their gospel throughout the world; but they have also a highly developed sense of their historic role as a great imperial power. Under Mao Tse-tung, we see the recrudescence of an age-old Chinese expansionism. As in Russia, so in China, communism rebuilt a decayed state and then provided the impetus for that state's dominance over others.

As early as the second century BC, the Chinese emperors forced several Burmese feudal states to pay tribute to them. It was only in the eighteenth century, when the Burmese defeated the Manchu rulers in bloody fights, that China's attempt to impose vassalage on them ended. But, even after that, the Chinese obstinately continued to claim that Burma was China's vassal.

The past 2,000 years of Vietnamese history are marked by China's determined efforts to incorporate part or the whole of Vietnam into China, countered by the equally determined resistance of the Vietnamese to Chinese encroachment. Vietnam's political relationship with China alternated between direct Chinese domination and indirect vassalage, until French control was established over Indochina in the nineteenth century. In addition to Burma and Vietnam, Manchu emperors also imposed tributary status on Laos, Siam and Korea.

The Chinese emperors were, of course, imperialists through and through. Their successors in Peking today now stand forth as our defenders against the modern imperialists. But, whatever hard words the new mandarins have to say about the *ancien régime* in China, they require full reverence from Chinese and foreigners alike for the achievements of the old China in their height, depth and breadth—particularly breadth. Every care is taken to ensure that later Chinese generations do not forget their solemn duty to the fatherland. In a middle-school textbook (*A Short History of Modern China*, edited by Liu Pei-hua and published in Peking in 1953), there is a 'Map of Chinese Territories Seized by Imperialism during the Period of Old Democratic Revolution, 1840–1919'. This map shows the areas once under Chinese domination or vassalage. Among the 'dependent' areas shown are: Nepal, Sikkim, Bhutan, Burma, North and South Vietnam, Laos, Cambodia, Malaya, Philippines, together with areas now in the Soviet Union. Since the argument that 'this area was once ours, therefore it is still ours' was good enough to warrant the conquest of Tibet and the aggression on India, it is not fanciful to believe that, when China thinks the moment ripe, she will attempt to annex her 'lost territories'. (See Map, pages 12–13.)

Pause for a moment to consider what a colossal confusion would result if every nation were to follow the policy of 'this was once mine, therefore it must again be mine'. France would put in a claim for the whole of England: didn't William the

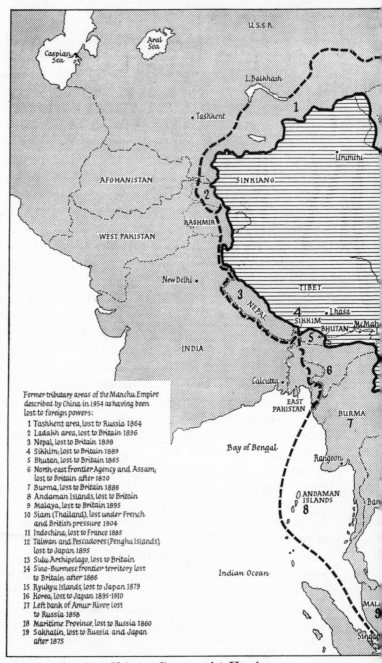

Former tributary areas of the Manchu Empire described by China in 1954 as having been lost to foreign powers:

1 Tashkent area, lost to Russia 1864
2 Ladakh area, lost to Britain 1896
3 Nepal, lost to Britain 1898
4 Sikkim, lost to Britain 1889
5 Bhutan, lost to Britain 1865
6 North-east frontier Agency and Assam, lost to Britain after 1820
7 Burma, lost to Britain 1886
8 Andaman Islands, lost to Britain
9 Malaya, lost to Britain 1895
10 Siam (Thailand), lost under French and British pressure 1904
11 Indochina, lost to France 1885
12 Taiwan and Pescadores (Penghu Islands), lost to Japan 1895
13 Sulu Archipelago, lost to Britain
14 Sino-Burmese frontier territory lost to Britain after 1886
15 Ryukyu Islands, lost to Japan 1879
16 Korea, lost to Japan 1895-1910
17 Left bank of Amur River, lost to Russia 1858
18 Maritime Province, lost to Russia 1860
19 Sakhalin, lost to Russia and Japan after 1875

Manchu Empire, Chinese Communist Version

Based on map published in *A Brief History of Modern China*, Peking 1953 (2nd edn 1954), which claims the numbered areas within the broken line to be 'Chinese territories prior to imperialist encroachment'.

Norman conquer it from Harold the Saxon? England, with
equal justice, would demand the restoration of the Angevin
empire, embracing half of France, and would make diplomatic
and military arrangements for the 'liberation' of the United
States, Canada, Australia and New Zealand and all the former
dominions and colonies of the British Crown. Not even China
herself would remain free: the Mongol descendants of Jenghiz
and Kublai Khan, and the rightful heirs of imperial Japan,
would be making their claims too. Where do we get with such
an absurd policy?

CONFLICT WITH INDIA

India's territorial boundary with China extends over 2,200
miles, and its entire length has either been defined by treaty
or recognised by custom and tradition. It follows the geo-
graphical principle of watersheds and is, in most places, the
crest of the Himalayas. This is the basic argument of the Indian
government. To this, the Chinese reply that 'the claim that the
entire Sino-Indian traditional customary boundary follows
well-known main watersheds is groundless'; and also that
'even though some sections of the Sino-Indian traditional
customary line may have comparatively distinct natural
features, it is necessary for the two sides to define jointly their
starting and terminal points and their specific alignments'.

Between October 1913 and July 1914, a tripartite conference
was held at Simla in India, attended by the representatives of
British India, China and Tibet. A treaty was signed at the
conclusion of the conference, demarcating the boundaries of
the three countries. The agreed boundary was called the
McMahon Line, after Sir Henry McMahon, the representative
of British India. Ivan Chen, the Chinese representative, signed
the Simla Convention and its attached map on his country's
behalf. This signature was later repudiated by the Chinese
government, but its objections, listed in four memoranda of
different dates (April 25, May 1 and June 13 in 1914, May 30

in 1919), were solely with regard to the boundary between Inner Tibet and China, and between Inner and Outer Tibet. China did not protest against the boundary between India and Tibet (now the Sino-Indian frontier), nor did it seek a modification of it after the Simla Convention.

Great was India's surprise when, forty years after the Simla Convention, the rulers of New China began to make provocative statements implying that the Sino-Indian boundary was not demarcated and that the McMahon Line was just some line arbitrarily drawn on the map by the British imperialists. When India pointed out the validity of the Simla documents, China replied that 'these documents are null and void', and that 'the Simla Conference did not discuss at all the question of delimiting the boundary between China and India'.

On June 25, 1954, Chou En-lai arrived in New Delhi on a state visit, and was welcomed by the Indian people with great shouts of *Hindi-Chini Bhai-Bhai* (Indians and Chinese are brothers). During this visit, the two prime ministers issued a joint statement in which they reaffirmed their faith in the Five Principles of Peaceful Coexistence, and also declared: 'If these Principles are applied, not only between various countries but also in international relations generally, they would form a solid foundation for peace and security and fears and apprehensions that exist today would give place to a feeling of confidence.'[1]

However, hardly had Chou returned home than Chinese patrols began to infiltrate into the disputed territory at Barahoti in Uttar Pradesh. On two occasions when the two men again met, Nehru pressed for an immediate and peaceful settlement of the border question. Chou En-lai evasively told him that there were practically no border problems, but what few there were could be settled amicably. The Indians, indeed, claim that, on a visit to India in November 1956, Chou even went so far as to say that the Chinese government proposed to recognise the McMahon Line in the case of the frontier with India, as it had already done in the case of the Sino-Burmese border.[2]

But, for all China's assurances of a peaceful settlement, the Indians discovered in 1957 that the Chinese had built a road linking Tibet to the province of Sinkiang which, for more than 100 miles, ran through territory claimed by India in the Aksai Chin.* Letters of protest flowed from the Indian government, with the usual evasive replies from China. The surprises, however, were not over. Peking published maps showing as part of China about 50,000 square miles of territory that India traditionally regards as her own. To India's renewed protests China replied that the new maps were reproductions of those that had existed for the past several decades, and that the new government had had no time to revise them. But Peking's true intentions may be judged from the fact that Chinese incursions continued even during the period when the officials appointed by the two governments to examine relevant documents were still meeting in Delhi, Rangoon and Peking.

While this dispute dragged on, the Tibetans rose in a national rebellion against Chinese rule. This rebellion was ruthlessly crushed and the Dalai Lama, supreme religious leader and 'God-king' of the Tibetans, fled to India for refuge. India's granting of asylum to the revered leader of the Tibetan people gave China new cause to intensify the campaign of vilification and pressure against India. Meanwhile, the infiltration of Chinese army patrols into the disputed territory continued until, on October 20, 1962, China threw off the thin veils covering her policy and launched a full-scale invasion of India. Thus did Mao and his government trample underfoot the Five Principles of Peaceful Coexistence which they had affirmed on so many occasions and—with brazen cynicism—were still to avow thereafter to Africa and other areas of the Third World.

* Some people argue that, since the road appears to have existed for about seven years before the Indians discovered it, this very fact strengthens China's claim to the area, India's ignorance being taken to invalidate India's sovereignty.

Nehru and his India, pioneers in applying the principles of peaceful coexistence in modern times, had believed, up to the last moment, in a peaceful solution. India was totally unprepared for war and it was only after the Chinese attack had begun that she made any serious attempt to arm in order to defend her territorial integrity and national honour.

China's purpose in attacking India is not completely clear. It may have been to humiliate this great country and thus make her appear less worthy to lead the Afro-Asian peoples. It may have been to slow down India's economic progress by forcing the government to divert a substantial portion of national resources to military purposes. China's policy probably embraced both these motives, together with the simple and blunt intention of establishing the New China's rights to all that the Old China had ever held at the height of its imperial power.

SUBJUGATION OF TIBET

Peking's leaders had, in fact, demonstrated very early in their regime what could be expected of the new communist expansionists. The agreement which contained the Five Principles in its preamble referred to the 'Tibet *region of* China'. Yet for many decades prior to the communist take-over in China, Tibet had been for all practical purposes an independent and sovereign country. Such foreign influence as existed there—and it was the minimum—was British rather than Chinese from 1911 onward. The Tibetans, in fact, did not allow China direct access to their country; Chinese who went to Tibet entered the country through India. An examination of the Peking communists' policy towards Tibet is most instructive for anyone who doubts the reality of Chinese expansionism.

On New Year's Day, 1950—exactly three months after the foundation of the People's Republic of China—Mao Tse-tung solemnly proclaimed to the Chinese people and the world that the 'liberation' of Tibet from imperialist aggression was the basic task of the People's Liberation Army. He at once

instituted an intense road-building programme and, on October
7 of the same year, the peace-loving Chinese forces, wielding
peaceful weapons, began the peaceful liberation of Tibet. Much
Tibetan blood got peacefully spilled in the process.

When Mao Tse-tung was struggling for power, he made the
Tibetans and all other minorities living within or contiguous
to China, a promise. On November 7, 1931, he said: 'The Soviet
government of China* recognises the right of self-determination
of the national minorities in China, their right of complete
separation from China, and the formation of an independent
state for each national minority.' Mao at that time needed the
help of these minorities in his revolutionary struggles and he
tried to offer them inducements.

The Tibetans belong to a different racial group from the
Chinese and they have developed a culture and tradition all
their own. In the eighth century, a treaty was concluded
between the rulers of Tibet and China which united the two
kingdoms. Later, in the thirteenth century, Kublai Khan, the
Mongol emperor, entrusted the administration of Tibet to the
Head Lama of the monastery of Sakya. The central Chinese
government, however, still controlled the collection of taxes
through its local governors in Tibet, and sanctioned the appoint-
ment of the Dalai Lama. The Tibetan people still enjoyed
internal autonomy, although under Chinese suzerainty. Under
a strong Chinese emperor, Tibet was ruled almost like a province
of China; under a weak one, on the other hand, the Tibetans
regained almost complete freedom.

The Tibetans' history, throughout the centuries, has been
marked by a strong yearning for independence. Except for two
short periods of direct Chinese rule—each of which ended in a
national revolt—Tibetan autonomy remained intact. Treaties
relating to Tibet, signed at different times, all explicitly recognised Tibetan autonomy as well as China's suzerainty. Lhalu,

* 'Soviet' is used here in the original meaning of 'revolutionary
council', and in this context does not relate specifically to the USSR.

one-time governor of Kham (in the eastern part of Tibet and nearest to China), related a story which will serve to show how strongly the Tibetans were opposed to any meddling in their internal affairs. 'When the Great Thirteenth [Dalai Lama] departed to the Heavenly Fields, some men of power wanted to betray Tibet to the Chinese. My father [commander-in-chief under the Thirteenth Dalai Lama] opposed them and sent defiant messages to Chiang Kai-shek, telling him to leave us alone.'[3] Had Tibet been an integral part of China, the question of betraying Tibet to the Chinese would not have arisen, nor would a commander-in-chief of the Tibetan army have defied Generalissimo Chiang by asking to be left alone. A year before his death, the Dalai Lama referred to by Lhalu drew up a Political Testament in which he wrote, among other things: 'The government of India is near to us and has a large army. The government of China also has a large army. We should therefore maintain firm friendship with these two; both are powerful.'[4] If Tibet had been an inseparable part of China, the Dalai Lama could hardly have contemplated such a policy.

From the Chinese view, the Tibetans had added insult to injury when, taking advantage of the confusion caused by the Chinese Civil War, they quietly expelled all Chinese officials and residents from Tibet. The International Commission of Jurists was later to say of this Tibetan action that it served to 'emphasise the fact that Tibet is re-established as a completely sovereign state, independent of China actually and legally'. The Tibetans, indeed, meant this gesture to emphasise their neutrality; the Chinese interpreted it as an affront.

The Chinese Red Army, during its 6,000-mile Long March in 1934, had to pass through the part of Tibet inhabited by Khamba and Mantzu tribesmen. The communist forces lost half of their number in this area, due to the determined harassment of these tribes. So implacable indeed were the Mantzu in their loathing for Chinese (of any political shade whatever) that their queen threatened to boil alive any of her subjects who helped the Red Army on its line of march. Mao Tse-tung never forgot this. His revenge came when the Red Army, now called the People's Liberation Army, returned to Tibet in October 1950.

Britain, during the time she held India, made some treaties which gave her rights in Tibet, and British military and para-military personnel were stationed there. India inherited these rights from Britain at independence in 1947, but indicated her willingness to relinquish them. By the time the Chinese moved against Tibet in 1950, the only Europeans there were Robert Ford, an English wireless operator in the service of the Tibetan government; an English missionary called Bull; Peter Auf-schnaiter, an Austrian engineer; Harrer, a German; and Nebdailoff, a White Russian. In the absence of any detailed explanation from the Chinese government, and in view of the total lack of evidence about 'imperialist occupation' or threat of invasion, it is difficult to conclude that these five Europeans represented a 'ferocious' threat of aggression, calling for China's liberation of Tibet.

China further justified the invasion by claiming Tibet as part of the 'motherland', which therefore should be reunited with it. This argument the Tibetans refused to accept and they resisted the Chinese. To Nehru's fervent appeals that the Tibetan question be settled by peaceful negotiation, China replied that she would indeed use only peaceful means. China's inter-pretation of 'peaceful means' was the dispatching of an army on a mission of 'liberation' on October 7, 1950.

By 1956, Tibetan armed resistance against the Chinese occupation had taken on fresh vigour, and a national rebellion began in March 1959. This was mercilessly crushed by the better armed and trained troops of the People's Liberation Army. But to all patriotic Tibetans, the words of General Kenchi Dawala still ring true: 'Tell the world we fought, and that we will fight again.'[5]

We in Africa should take to heart the lesson of Tibet. The Red Chinese are irreproachable in their expressions of love for freedom. So much do they abhor the oppression of one people by another, and so much indeed do they sympathise with all oppressed peoples, that they are fully prepared to come and liberate us—even without our express invitation. From such ardent freedom-lovers one would have expected reparation of the injustice done by the Chinese emperors. One would have expected the freedom-loving 'new' Chinese to endorse for the Tibetans that independence for which they had for ever yearned and for which they have shed their blood for generations. But when Tibet claimed that independence, China's answer was the bayonets of its army.

As for the reparation of injustice: we should do well in Africa to be most wary when the Chinese talk to us of 'justice'. In June 1959, the International Commission of Jurists in Geneva published a report which indicted the Chinese authorities in Tibet for the violation of most of the human rights proclaimed by the United Nations. A team of legal experts spent two months in collecting and sifting evidence from Tibetan refugees. Their conclusions may be summarised thus:

1. From 1950 onwards, an independent country was turned by force into a province of China.

2. The terms of the agreement of 1951, guaranteeing a broad measure of autonomy to Tibet, had been consistently flouted by the Chinese.

3. There had been arbitrary confiscation of property belonging to monasteries, individuals and the Tibetan government.

4. Freedom of religion had been denied, the Chinese authorities attempting all in their power to destroy the Tibetan Buddhist religion, its monasteries, shrines and monuments. A campaign of Communist indoctrination and bitterly anti-religious propaganda had been launched.

5. The Tibetans had been denied all freedom of information.

6. There had been a systematic policy of killing, imprison-
ing and deporting those opposed to the Communist regime.
According to reliable sources, the total number of people
killed had reached 65,000.

The report accused the Chinese government of genocide as
defined by the 1948 Genocide Convention of the United Nations.
It said that there was 'a *prima facie* case that on the part of the
Chinese there has been an attempt to destroy the national
ethnic, racial and religious group of Tibetans as such' by killing
some members of the group and by causing serious bodily and
mental harm to others.

Some friends of China have argued that, because the Tibetan
nation was backward, China was right in conquering it and
hustling its people into the twentieth century. We colonial and
former colonial peoples have ineradicable memories of such
arguments. The argument of 'civilising mission' and 'cultural
superiority' went hand-in-hand in Africa in the last century
with conquering swords and fraudulent treaties. A similar
argument of 'superiors' over 'inferiors' was considered valid by
the followers of Mohammed when they took up arms to win
converts for the prophet. In all ages, it has been an argument
masking brutality and greed. In our day, the alleged superiority
of the communist system has been advanced to justify forcing
it on unwilling peoples by every conceivable foul means. Seeing
the amount of suffering and misery that this argument has
brought upon the world, it is an affront to our human understanding and dignity to produce it as an excuse for aggression
against weaker peoples, such as that of China against the Tibetans.

Occupied Tibet has sunk into silence. Under the direct heel
of Chinese military rule, the Tibetan people today have not
even a nominal government of their own. The Dalai Lama,
forced to flee into exile, is denounced by Peking as a 'traitor'.
Even the Panchen Lama, who was set up by the Chinese as
their puppet, has outlived his usefulness to them. Removed

from such shadowy dignity as was given him by Peking, he is now locked away somewhere as the leader of a 'reactionary clique'

Such is the lesson of Tibet.

SUBORNING INDIA'S NEIGHBOURS

Other countries close to India have also felt the hot breath of the Dragon rather than the gentle air of peaceful coexistence.

Burma had enough goodwill towards China to have been the first country in the world to recognise the Peking government. But hardly two years passed before the Burmese were faced with Chinese military pressure on their frontiers. China published maps showing four disputed areas as Chinese territory, and skirmishes took place when Peking attempted to settle the dispute by force. Fortunately for Burma, other pressing matters made China modify her plans, and the Sino-Burmese border dispute was hastily settled according to the internationally recognised principle of watershed delineation.

Nepal, situated between India and Tibet, was invaded and defeated by the Chinese in the late eighteenth century. The Nepalese were forced to accept China's suzerainty and, until 1910, paid tribute to China every five years. Nepal, in its turn, established a hold over Tibet in the mid-nineteenth century, and the Tibetans paid yearly tribute to Nepal, in addition to granting to their conquerors certain extraterritorial rights. Nepal gave up her demand for annual tribute from Tibet after the Chinese communist regime had consolidated its position there, and also relinquished her extraterritorial rights.

Despite these obvious signs of Nepal's goodwill, China continued to claim parts of Nepalese territory, including the whole of Mount Everest. When the Nepalese would not yield, China concentrated troops on the frontier and subjected this little Himalayan kingdom to systematic intimidation. Chinese troops opened fire on Nepalese border guards in July 1960, killing one and wounding several others. This incident so shook the Nepalese that King Mahendra rushed post-haste to settle the border problem with Peking. China later relinquished her claim to the southern half of Mount Everest, and the two parties demarcated the boundary according to internationally accepted principles. Why was this not done in the first place? Ask the Chinese, who apparently found it suited their policy to terrorise their neighbour and shed blood before sitting down at the conference table.

Bhutan, like Nepal, lies along the now dangerous frontiers of the Himalayas. In 1958, China laid claim to 300 square miles of territory that the Bhutanese traditionally regarded as theirs. When fighting broke out between India and China in 1962, the Chinese forcibly passed through this territory in order to reach the rear of the Indian troops in the North East Frontier Agency.

Having failed to win over to its side the Prime Minister of Bhutan, Jigme Dorji, Peking sought allies among his opponents and plotted his overthrow by violence. In March 1964, Dorji was assassinated. His murderer, Jambay Dukpa, was found in possession of two pistols and seven hand-grenades. He confessed that he had been instructed to wipe out Dorji's whole family, and that he and his fellow-conspirators were helped by the Chinese. Peking's aim was to take advantage of the political confusion caused by Dorji's murder, which occurred while the King of Bhutan was absent in Europe for medical treatment, and thereby orientate the country towards China. Fortunately for this small Himalayan state, the King left Europe and reached his country in time to get the situation under tolerable control.

◙   ◙

Such, in brief, is China's record in dealing with her neighbours in the light of the solemnly proclaimed Five Principles. Against Burma, Nepal and Bhutan (and, we may add, Sikkim), it is a record of bullying pressure from without and subversion from within. Against India, it is war of aggrandisement. Against Tibet, bloody conquest and unremitting oppression.

This is the record of the China who joins us in condemning the

Portuguese colonialists in Angola, but pursues a savage colonialist policy of her own nearer home.

When Chou En-lai made his 'grand tour' of Africa in 1963–64, he cited ancient historical ties which, he said, should be the cause and basis for the eternal friendship between African and Chinese peoples. Fine. Africa is weak and poor, and Africa needs friends. But what kind of friends?

Push ideology aside for a while. If there is any country with which China should want to maintain friendly relations for historical and other reasons, that country is India. Beginning from AD 65, a regular stream of Buddhist missionaries—including such famous scholars as Kashyapa Matanga Kumarajiva, Dharma Kshema and Paramartha—flowed from India into China. In the opposite direction came equally famous men, among them Fa-Hien, Hiuan-Tsang and I-Tsing. At the same time, Indian and Chinese traders maintained brisk contact by land and sea. Contact became less frequent after the eleventh century, but was actively renewed after the victory of the Chinese revolution in 1911. When Japan invaded China, the Indians sent a medical mission as a mark of their solidarity with the Chinese. India was among the first countries to recognise the new People's Republic of China in 1949. Since then, India has on every possible occasion pressed for the admission of Communist China to the United Nations, and has spoken up for her neighbour at international gatherings, sometimes to the detriment of her own interests. Add to all this the Five Principles of Peaceful Coexistence which the two countries adopted in 1954 and reaffirmed at Bandung a year later.

On the African side of the scale, put a few pieces of ancient and very broken Chinese porcelain found somewhere or other on the East African coast. Add Admiral Cheng Ho's voyages to our eastern shores to gather ivory, parrots and 'devil slaves'

All India's ancient and modern ties with China, and all Nehru's sincerest efforts at coexistence could not move the Chinese to treat India in a just and civilised manner. So I ask:

On what grounds does Africa expect better treatment from China than India got?

Africa has (and let us be thankful!) no contiguous frontier with China, and certainly it is not easy to imagine the Chinese coming half-way round the world in order to seize territory in Africa. But that is not the important point. The important point is that China is branded with the marks of duplicity and treachery. Africa could be betrayed in a hundred ways by such a country.

The most grievous mistake India made in her relations with China was the failure to put her foot down—hard—as soon as it was apparent that China was becoming intolerable. But that mistake may be excused on the grounds that India sincerely believed that the leaders of New China had repudiated the imperialism of the Old China. India has been betrayed and humiliated. If her ordeal does not reveal to us the true colours of New China, then India's suffering has been in vain.

It seems to me that we Africans should have become more wary of Communist China just *because* the Chinese soft-speakers made such neat lists of their 'principles' for dealing with Africa. On the record, many of China's bad deeds have been preceded by itemised good words. In the case of Nepal, for example, as soon as a neat document was drawn up, covering trade relations among other things, 90 per cent of the traditional Nepalese traders in Tibet were expelled and every sort of restriction was put in the way of the few who remained. Then a road-building agreement was concluded, with Chinese engineers and workers coming into Nepal to build the first road link ever to be forged between the Himalayan kingdom of Nepal and the Chinese communist 'colony' of Tibet. Once the road was done—and what peaceful purpose could it have served if not trade?—the last trade ties between Nepal and China's Tibet were severed.

◫   ◫

But, it might be said, Peking's record of perfidy could be something in the experience of non-Chinese alone. Let's take a look.

While in high school in 1912, Mao Tse-tung managed to organise the students into a union, though he was repeatedly threatened with expulsion for fomenting strikes. Thus united, the students could insist on better food and even on some measure of freedom. But the same Mao, as soon as he came to power, banned all free speech and political activity, and any form of association except under the Communist Party's aegis, with the result that now, when the people still eat poor food and have next to no personal freedom, they have no means of agitating for improvement. Freedom of association and agitation for one's rights were good things when Mao and his henchmen were struggling for power. Today, Mao and his men have reached the pinnacle of their dreams, and anyone who agitates for better food or more freedom of speech or of association is a 'reactionary', a 'counter-revolutionary', an 'enemy of the people' meriting immediate liquidation.

In 1957, Mao invited the Chinese people to speak their minds freely. With the words, 'Let a Hundred Flowers bloom, let a Hundred Schools contend', he permitted the masses to criticise his party's policies the way people do elsewhere as a matter of course and as of right. Then, with the gale-force of seven years of pent-up feeling, criticism and complaints blew through the length and breadth of the land, leaving behind them ideological confusion and devastation. Said a college professor: 'Today, we do not even know the height or size of a person we elect, let alone his character or ability. We have simply become ballot-casting machines.'[6] Said two students of Chinese literature in a poem entitled *The time has come*: 'The time has come to demand freedom from the Communists. . . .' In Hunan province alone in the month of July, the peasants—the people said to be so much in love with the new regime—staged 320 riots and demonstrations against the party. At least twenty-seven anti-communist organisations were reported in eleven provinces by the official press.

Then, suddenly, came the political autumn, and then the

winter—all by the party's orders. The Hundred Flowers of free speech wilted, withered, dropped, and were trampled under foot by the Chinese Communist Party.

Spread over vast tracts of China are the national minorities —Uigurs, Kazakhs, Miaos, Mongols and many others—belonging to racial groups distinct from the Hans, the true Chinese. As we have already noted in connection with the Tibetans, Mao Tse-tung made these minorities a promise in 1931 when he was struggling for power: that they would have the right of self-determination. Mao got what he wanted, the support—or at least the neutrality—of the national minorities in his bid for power. You know what the Tibetans got when they dared to claim 'the right of self-determination' and 'complete separation from China'. Other minorities have shared the Tibetan experience. Today, Peking will stand no nonsense about self-determination and independence. New China's constitution carries a clause which reads: 'Each national autonomous region is an integral part of the People's Republic of China.' You may think that 'national autonomous region' sounds fine. It is indeed a very fine phrase, and one that Peking for good reason uses in preference to the more accurate term of 'Chinese-dominated colony'. Thus has closed yet another chapter in Peking's volume of broken promises.

Loudest among the promises the Chinese Communist Party made to the people of China before the 'liberation' was the pledge that they would regain the freedoms snatched away from them by despotic rulers and landlords. Against this promise is to be set the governing principle of the communist regime in Peking, that principle which is best defined in Mao Tse-tung's celebrated statement that 'political power grows out of the barrel of a gun'. Faithfully followed in China's policy towards her neighbours, it has certainly not been retracted in the policy of Mao and his colleagues towards their own people. They have demonstrated it by managing their country by a policy of sheer force. When I was there in 1962–63, the 'shooting stage' seemed over, and yet I met no one who did not show signs of a fear of punishment if he so much as expressed one word or gesture that was out of line with 'party policy'. There is still argument about whether 2,800 000 persons were liquidated after the communist take-over or whether it was 'only 750,000', as Mao claimed in 1957.

When he stated this figure, Mao was defending the policies of his party against the accusations of those who made criticisms during the 'Hundred Flowers' period of frank speaking. The argument was settled by force in that those who spoke out to question were silenced rather than answered. Only a few were shot this time. Tens of millions were merely 'sent down' to more humble positions to 'learn from the masses'. Professors became floor-sweepers of university buildings, so that their colleagues could see the degradation of their one-time peers and thus learn their own lesson. Spirited students became carters of manure in rural communes. By the time I arrived in Peking, 'going down' had taken on a grimmer meaning for students than that associated with the same term in universities of the English tradition. Some had gone down and returned, sadder and wiser in the ways of the party; some remained 'down'; others trembled in fear of being 'sent down'. It was a terrible punishment: a penitential way of life forced on 'dissident elements' as surely as if the impetus grew out of the barrel of a gun.

The end is not yet. In the late summer of 1966, the Red Guards movement ran amok—but controlled from above, you may be sure, not spontaneously—to destroy whatever spark of independent judgement still survived within the party and among the people as a whole.

China's rulers promised freedom and justice to the Chinese. They cannot keep even these promises made to their own people. What guarantee is there that they will be any more faithful to us in Africa?

Let Africa seek friends by all means. But let them be friends we can trust.

TWO

Peking's Theory of War and Peace

As both Emperor Haile Selassie of Ethiopia and President Bourguiba of Tunisia frankly told the Chinese Premier on his African tour, one of the fundamental points of disagreement between Africa and China is the question of war and peace. It is not at all clear whom Chou En-lai thought he was fooling when he said in his Principle Two that 'China supports the pursuance of a policy of peace'. It is worth our while to examine China's theory of what is peace and what war.

But first we need to see the precept and practice of Peking in the general context of the communist theory of war. Lenin said: 'War is an inevitable part of capitalism. It is just as much a legitimate form of capitalism as is peace. . . . It is simply insane to talk about abolishing capitalism without a frightful civil war or without a succession of such wars.'[1] These words—which seem to me to be saying, in fact, that war is an inevitable part of communist socialism—are echoed repeatedly by China. What sense can we make of them?

Let's start with the first part of the statement: 'War is an inevitable part of capitalism.' In my opinion, this is a political fallacy that has been lent a semblance of truth by frequent repetition. It is as a result of accepting this same fallacy that most Africans tend to confuse capitalism with imperialism, and thus draw the entirely erroneous conclusion that a non-capitalist political system is necessarily non-imperialist. This, of course, is what Lenin implied in his statement.

Certain Africans have tried to lend substance to the Leninist argument by some rather wild-eyed theorising. Nkrumah's *Neo-Colonialism: The Last Stage of Imperialism* was not, however, African. It is known to have been 'ghost-written' by 'a committee of five of Nkrumah's advisers, not one of whom was African. Moreover, the book was so glaringly biased that no objective person could take it seriously. As a reviewer in the *West African Pilot* (Lagos, December 22, 1965) said of it: 'That Nkrumah has allowed this serious bias to pass uncorrected can only confirm the charge often levelled at him by many African colleagues, that he is already too tight in the grip of the Eastern neo-colonialists.'

The African tendency to associate capitalism and imperialism is, of course, understandable. Not so long ago, all the significant imperialist powers were capitalist, and it would have been difficult at any time before the Second World War to imagine a non-capitalist imperialist. But recent history has shown that imperialism is by no means a monopoly of the capitalists. In fact, some newly emergent socialist countries have shown an alarming propensity to imperialism. China herself is a notorious example. The experiences of Tibet, India, Burma, Bhutan and Nepal, already described here, reveal in China's activities an especially militant brand of imperialism.

Lenin should have lived to eat up his own words at the sight of China and the Soviet Union—two indisputably socialist countries in Lenin's meaning—strengthening the border defences along their common frontier.

In the mid-eighteenth century, the armies of His Imperial Majesty Ch'ien Lung conquered a vast area between the Tian

Shan (Mountains of Heaven) and Tibet. The area was named Sinkiang—the New Dominion—and was incorporated into the Manchu empire. The original inhabitants of Sinkiang were Uzbeks, Kazakhs, Mongols, Tatars and other non-Han nationalities.* After the victory of the communist revolution in China, large numbers of Chinese were transplanted to the area, partly to counter-balance the political and economic influence the Russians had gained in this region at the time when China's national dynamism was at its weakest. But this policy of colonisation was also in full consonance with traditional Han arrogance toward national minorities. Mao Tse-tung put it concretely in an address to the Supreme State Council in 1957: 'Less than 5 per cent of the people in China occupy more than half of our territory. They are tribesmen, once not regarded as part of the Chinese race. We must convert them and convince them that they are Chinese.'

The minority races deeply resented the measures introduced by the new regime: measures which included an attempt to stamp out their religions. The Russians fanned minority discontent as best they could in the Chinese areas close to Russian frontiers, even going so far as to supply arms to the dissident minorities. There followed revolt after revolt against Chinese rule. About 50,000 minority nationals are reported to have crossed the border into the Soviet Union after an outbreak of bridge demolition and general sabotage. The first border skirmishes occurred in 1960, and the situation along the frontier has remained very uneasy since then. The Chinese have published maps showing the border as 'undemarcated'. As to what may follow, your guess is as good as mine. What concerns all of us in this matter is that the consequences of the Sino-Soviet frontier dispute could be war, as has happened elsewhere over disputed borders. And the fact that two

* Han, a Chinese dynasty (206 BC–AD 220), is the term used to identify the relatively 'pure Chinese' in distinguishing them from the various minority groups of different ethnic background.

'fraternal socialist countries' are involved does not speak in favour of Lenin's argument. Moreover, it clearly refutes the communist claim that they uphold peaceful coexistence, for the two greatest communist states cannot even coexist peacefully with one another!

The second part of Lenin's statement is as false as the first. Many countries, once wholly capitalist, have come under socialist governments without any 'frightful civil war'. Denmark, Norway and Sweden are just a few examples. The fact that neither the Chinese nor the Russians will allow these countries to be socialist (simply because they are not communist socialist) should not blind us to the significance of this. The important point is that these people have political systems which are socialist in respect to the fundamental aims of socialism—democratic government, equal opportunity, and the welfare of all citizens—whether or not they conform to the Moscow or the Peking formula.

The Chinese assert that 'wherever the country or place, where one finds oppression, there one finds resistance'. This statement is meant as a justification of China's revolutionary war theory. I grant that, though not always true, it is far more sensible than Lenin's theory quoted above. The general conclusion of the Chinese statement is that oppression favours the outbreak of wars, since the oppressed peoples are likely to take up arms to fight for their lost freedom. If we call Hungary to witness, Lenin's capitalist-imperialist theory gets us nowhere. In 1956, the Hungarians said loudly and plainly that all they wanted was to be left alone, but Khrushchev and his Soviet tank commanders thought otherwise. Hungary was crushed. Unless the Soviets will agree to be classified with the capitalists, Lenin's statement is obviously false. The Chinese statement, whether this be its intention or not, by inference puts the Soviet Union in the category of oppressors.

It is not unfair, I think, to employ the familiar communist device of capturing and turning the enemy's own guns against

53024

him. If we are to judge from the large number of revolts and simmering rebellions that have erupted against Chinese rule in the province of Sinkiang; if we are to judge from the national revolt of Tibet in 1959 and from the continued resistance of Khamba tribesmen in the Tibetan mountains; if we consider the volcanic reaction of the Chinese masses and the intelligentsia during the brief 'Hundred Flowers' campaign—how can we conclude other than that there is oppression even in peace-loving, socialist China? Since armed hostilities have actually occurred in some of these cases, I see no basis for Lenin's theory of isolating capitalism as the warmongering force in the world.

Imperialism breeds war. But since imperialism is not the exclusive preserve of any one political system, wars may be provoked by any camp: capitalist, socialist, neutralist, or the unclassified and unclassifiable. What this world needs is not pseudo-scientific analyses of what camp is likely to provoke the next war. What we need is goodwill in our divergences. Hate the other man's politics and all his other beliefs if you think you must, but don't cut his throat because of his politics and beliefs. That is what I understand by peaceful coexistence. That is what the great majority of people in the world mean by peaceful coexistence. It is not, to our woe, what the Chinese communists believe.

◻　　　　　　◻

The Chinese have consistently maintained that war is inevitable while capitalism* and socialism exist side by side, and that the day wars will cease will be the day when capitalism has ceased to exist and socialism holds unchallenged sway in the world. Well and good. But in view of the fact that capitalist countries consider their own system, as it is at present, to be far superior to what Chinese socialism offers, and will therefore not go into

* The term they actually use here is 'imperialism', in this being faithful to Lenin's theory that imperialism is an inevitable manifestation of the capitalism described by Marx.

voluntary liquidation; and since for their part the Chinese communists are prepared to go to all lengths to promote their system, it becomes clear that the regime in Peking will never abandon the policy of 'peace through war' until such time as all the world has become socialist, as China defines socialism. The *People's Daily* made this quite clear when it declared in December 1962: 'As to the assertion that it is possible to create a "world without war", this is certainly absolute nonsense.'

How do these attitudes accord with the peaceful coexistence that Chou En-lai preached on our continent?

For years after the Second World War, suspicion and mutual distrust between the Western and the Eastern camps were so intense that each side thought the best way to deter the other from unleashing a war was to pile up more and more arms of the most lethal kind. It was during this period that the expressions 'cold war', 'arms race' and 'we will bury you' became current in the political vocabulary of all the major languages. Indeed, there came a moment—the Cuban crisis of October 1962— when we all thought the funeral hour of the civilised world was at hand. But good sense prevailed in Washington and Moscow, and the Soviets withdrew their missiles from America's 'doorstep'. Tension eased, and the world breathed again with relief. No, not all the world. There was one country which thought— and still thinks—that all wars, both hot and cold, can be of positive benefit in the struggle to liquidate those it hates. That country wrung its hands in sore disappointment when Khrushchev withdrew from the brink. In its disappointment, that country accused the Soviet Union of 'capitulating' to American imperialism. That country was the People's Republic of China.

Mao Tse-tung was reported to have said in 1958 that, though the West thinks it will profit from it, the cold war 'is more profitable to our [socialist] countries'. The report of the third plenary session of the central committee of the Costa Rica People's Vanguard Party, meeting at about this time, stated: 'In talks on the question of international policy, the Chinese leaders told our comrades that the "cold war is a good thing", and that the "situation of tension is a good situation" for the development of the revolutionary struggle.'[2]

While elevating force to first place, Mao also glosses over the difference between various kinds of force. His attitude towards nuclear power, for example, is unique. 'The atom bomb is a paper tiger which the United States reactionaries use to scare people', says Mao. 'It looks terrible, but in fact it is not.'[3]

The *People's Daily* elaborated this pronouncement by pointing out in one of its editorials that revolutionary victories were won in Korea, Vietnam, Cuba and Algeria despite the fact that the opposing camp possessed atom bombs. The Chinese found it convenient to conceal the fact that, in the instances cited, the use of the bomb by any side was neither tactically nor strategically desirable. Even so, can we discount the danger of 'local wars' escalating into global wars in which the nuclear powers take opposite sides? Cuba could have been a case in point. Khrushchev said he sent his missiles there because of reports of an impending invasion by Cuban exiles based in the United States. Had that 'local' invasion taken place when Russian missiles were on the island . . . the mind staggers!

Even more outrageous is another statement of Mao's. When discussing the question of what proportion of the world's population would perish in the event of a nuclear war, he said:

> I had an argument about this with Nehru. In this respect he was more pessimistic than I am. I told him that, if half of humanity is destroyed, the other half will still remain, but imperialism will be destroyed entirely and there will be only socialism in all the world; and within half a century, or a whole century, the population will again increase by more than half.[4]

These are the words of the man who controls the lives and destiny of 700 million Chinese: the man who now invites the peoples of Africa, Asia and Latin America to rally under his protective wing.

If half the people of the world must perish according to Mao's formula, that half is at least entitled to say whether it consents to perish *so that communist socialism may triumph*. Each and all of us have the right to say whether the brand of socialism Mao is peddling is worth perishing for in the first place. And what of the other half: those who, having survived the first blasts, will face a slow and agonising death, and whose children will be still-born or born with unimaginable deformities? They too have the right to a choice in the matter. But it is not surprising that Mao should not bother himself to consult those whom he marks out for sacrifice on the altar of his socialism. The principle of free choice got forgotten in China when the communists came to power.

The late Secretary-General of the Italian Communist Party, Palmiro Togliatti, expressed his fears to a high Chinese official. Togliatti thought that, in the event of a nuclear war, all Italy would be wiped out. The Chinese official tried to brush away his fears with the words: 'But other people would remain, and imperialism would be destroyed.'[5] On another occasion, a Czechoslovakian journalist pointed out to Tao Chu, a member of the Central Committee of the Chinese Communist Party, that all the thirteen million Czechs could be wiped out in a thermonuclear war. Tao Chu told him: 'In the case of a war of annihilation, the small countries belonging to the socialist camp would have to subordinate their interests to the common interests of the entire camp as a whole.'[6] Cold comfort will it be to the Italians and the Czechs to get 'buried' so that China's five-starred banner might flutter in the four winds of the world.

We in Africa have an intimate interest in peace and in the elimination of the cold war. We do not believe, as do the Chinese, that we can afford to postpone economic reconstruction, to resume it after the nuclear world war. We know that, if there were no arms race, more aid would be available to us from the great powers to promote that rapid development of our countries which is one of our most cherished goals. We know that, in the event of a third world war, the use of nuclear weapons is a dreadful probability. And we know, too, that even if no part of Africa is directly bombed, the resulting radio-active fall-out will not respect our frontiers.

Even the United States, the richest nation on earth, has recognised the need to start a campaign against poverty *in the United States*. When I was in Siberia, in the spring of 1962, I had cause to wonder seriously whether the Siberians were also part of that nation which could afford to explode 50-megaton bombs, so much did their living conditions fall short of what I expected of the nation that had launched the sputnik. It is characteristic of the Chinese leaders that they should think little of the welfare of the masses for whose benefit they claim to rule. Foreign Minister Chen Yi stated flatly that China would have atom bombs 'even if the people have to go without trousers'. That is why the minds of China's rulers always run in grooves that lead towards more cold war, more revolutionary wars, and more nuclear bombs, when their major concern should be more rice for empty bellies and more clothes for bare backs. It is only to people whose hearts are devoid of all sympathy for their fellow men that the tense international situation can be 'a good thing'.

Probably the one most significant and hopeful development in East-West relations was the signing of the partial nuclear test-ban treaty in August 1963. Men of many nations and of varying ideologies hailed it as the first step toward the time when, despite diverse beliefs and practices, all men can live in a world without war. But China came out against this as vitu-peratively as ever, labelling the test-ban treaty as a 'deception', as 'treason', and as a 'conspiracy of the imperialists'.

I should have liked to believe that the Chinese government was sincere when, in July 1963, it proclaimed its programme for the 'complete prohibition and destruction of nuclear weapons

and all means of delivering them to their targets'. Total disarmament (the whole loaf) must be the goal. Yet this does not
make the partial test-ban (a half-loaf) any less desirable. It
was the first really hopeful sign that the antagonisms between
East and West could be regulated by a measure of common
sense.

Many of the African leaders whom Chou En-lai and Chen Yi
met during their 1963–64 tour were bothered by the Chinese
antagonism to the test-ban treaty. And no matter how expertly
the Chinese spokesmen 'explained' and rationalised, doubts
about the Chinese intentions remained. Some of the African
leaders suspected that this slight indication of a lessening of
tensions between East and West was actually anathema to
China, for whose policies it was essential that the antagonisms
should grow rather than lessen.

And all the time the Chinese leaders were preaching 'complete
prohibition of nuclear weapons', and attacking the United
States and its allies as evil nuclear powers (while at the same
time bidding us 'underdeveloped' populations not to fear the
'imperialist paper tiger'), what was China actually doing?
Developing her own 'paper tiger', of course.

The explosion of China's first nuclear device, on October 16,
1964, followed within a few days the end of the Conference of
Non-Aligned States in Cairo. It was a contemptuous reply to
the conference's appeal to all states to sign the test-ban treaty
and renounce the manufacture of nuclear weapons. Peking
stated on the day of the explosion that it was 'a major achievement of the Chinese people in their struggle to increase their
national defence capability'. Most significant was the Chinese
claim that 'the mastering of the nuclear weapon by China is a
great encouragement to the revolutionary peoples of the world
in their struggles, and a great contribution to the cause of
defending world peace'.

This view was not widely shared! U Thant, Secretary-General
of the United Nations, expressed the general opinion when he

said the test was 'deplorable' and 'particularly regrettable in the wake of the signing last year of the partial nuclear test-ban treaty which was endorsed by the General Assembly by an overwhelming majority'. In the communist world, the only expressions of satisfaction came from Albania, North Korea and North Vietnam, and from the Indonesian Communist Party.

In the teeth of almost universal revulsion, the Chinese insisted that they were as keen as ever on the prohibition and destruction of nuclear weapons. But how keen Peking really is about this was shown by its refusal to come to a disarmament conference. The *People's Daily* commented on November 22, 1964:

> It is more difficult for the Geneva disarmament conference to solve the question of a complete prohibition of nuclear weapons than for a camel to pass through the needle's eye. . . .
>
> We thank the us government for its 'generosity' in not opposing China's participation in the Geneva disarmament conference, but we must tell it frankly that it will not have the pleasure of our company.

And yet the Chinese government asserts that 'the Chinese people can be trusted' with nuclear weapons, and reiterates the slogan that 'nuclear arms in China's hands are only for safeguarding world peace'. The Indian government, made wise by bitter experience, summed up the worth of Chinese assurances in its Note to Peking of February 16, 1965, at a time when reports were circulating of a second nuclear explosion by China. After pointing out that the first test had flouted the opinion of forty-seven non-aligned countries, India reminded Peking that it had supported the declaration of the 1955 Bandung Conference which appealed to all powers to agree to suspend nuclear tests. China 'thus stands condemned in terms of her own solemn commitment'.

The most frightening aspect of China's attitude towards

nuclear power (and she is pressing on with nuclear tests) is the fact that her leaders still appear to underestimate the threat of this fantastic force. They still talk about 'paper tigers' and profess no hesitation about taking whatever risks they deem desirable in coyly tempting nuclear war. There had been opinion among some Western scientists that China's rash attitude would become more sober when she learned more about nuclear power through her own experience with it. So far, however, this prediction seems to have been overoptimistic.

The Chinese leaders' attitude toward negotiation in connection with nuclear weapons also has not become any more realistic than it was in 1964 when they refused to participate in the Geneva disarmament talks. After China's third test, her spokesman revealed that China had offered the United States an agreement under which both countries would pledge themselves not to use nuclear weapons first. Considering the relative power held by the two sides of such an agreement the Chinese 'offer' is of course ludicrous. The United States, with an army smaller than China's, presumably has a formidable stock of nuclear weapons (which leads to all the argument about 'overkill'), while China has millions of men under arms and neither weapons nor a delivery system for weapons. I do not mean, by pointing out these facts, to underestimate the Chinese bomb; I am very frightened of it, in fact, because I am a person who knows from first-hand experience how tough the Chinese can be. I just wish to point out that, under present circumstances, the Chinese offer of a 'deal' with the United States is transparent nonsense.

How soon China will be in a position to translate her nuclear potential into deliverable weapons is not certain. What is certain is that the acquisition of a nuclear potential will intensify, not moderate, Peking's policy for dominating where she can and provoking instability and disorder where she cannot dominate. One of her motives in pressing forward with nuclear bomb research while calling for nuclear disarmament was manifestly to strengthen her position *vis-à-vis* Russia. China is now waging two cold wars: one against the West and the other against the Soviet Union.

We Africans must be the most concerned about our place in China's struggle against the two big powers. Unfortunately, the Chinese spokesmen have made our African role distressingly clear. We fit neatly into the Maoist tactics of guerrilla warfare as it applies on an international basis. What does this mean? Defence Minister Lin Piao explained it in these words:

> Comrade Mao Tse-tung's theory of the establishment of rural revolutionary base areas and the encirclement of the cities from the countryside is of outstanding and universal practical importance for the present revolutionary struggles. . . . Taking the entire globe, if North America and Western Europe can be called 'the cities of the world', then Asia, Africa, and Latin America constitute 'the rural areas of the world'. . . . In the final analysis, the whole cause of world revolution hinges on the revolutionary struggles of the Asian, African, and Latin American peoples. . . . The socialist countries should regard it as their internationalist duty to support the people's revolutionary struggles in Asia, Africa, and Latin America.

So we see that it has become the 'internationalist duty' of China to support the revolutionary struggle which will overcome the industrialised West—and presumably the industrialised USSR as well. What if we people of the 'rural areas' of the world do not want to fight such a fight? China obviously intends to see that we *do* want to fight it, because her leaders recognise its importance and know that the best way to fight any war is to let the other fellow do it for you. Lin Piao reassures us that the struggle can be won:

> The struggles waged by the different peoples against US imperialism reinforce each other and merge into a world-

wide tide of opposition. . . . Everything is divisible. And so is this colossus of US imperialism. It can be split up and defeated. The peoples of Asia, Africa, and Latin America and other regions can destroy it piece by piece. . . .

The Vietnamese people know the meaning of this 'piece by piece' struggle in which not one Chinese has so far lost his life.

Every conflict between African nations, or between factions within African nations, contributes to the Chinese purpose of spreading chaos and confusion to keep the 'imperialists' off balance. I am sure we Africans could help keep the Western imperialists 'off balance', but what would happen to us meanwhile? Our small populations could be decimated while China's 700 million people peacefully reproduce. The concept of the international application of Mao's guerrilla tactics is hardly designed to appeal to Africans.

Regardless of this fact, Chou and Chen toured Africa in 1963–64 to sell the idea that the continent is 'ripe for revolution'. Of course, they did not openly say this everywhere. Sometimes they spoke eloquently about peace, but the sum of their words carried enough belligerence to alert African leaders. Chou's little sentence spoken in Somalia—'revolutionary prospects are excellent throughout the African continent'—drew more fire from both African and non-African sources than did all the routine condemnations of the imperialists by one whose country is so manifestly representative of that species.

China in the late nineteenth and early twentieth centuries was a country debilitated by civil wars and imperial negligence and misrule. Like hungry wolves, many comparatively strong powers—Japan, Britain, France, Tsarist Russia and several others—pounced on this weakling and subjected her to many humiliations. Under the circumstances, it is natural that the new China that emerged from such sore trials should feel persecuted, hated and encircled. For such a country, self-preservation and the restoration of national dignity should obviously be cardinal policies. But there is every evidence that the new China that was born in 1949 has carried these policies too far, to the extent that even erstwhile friends—India, the Soviet Union and Indonesia, to mention just three—have now become enemies against whom China must prepare to defend herself. Had Tibet never been touched, had there been no war with India, and had there been no threat to weaker countries around, would not the rest of the world have recognised the new China's new-found peaceful intentions and sought to reciprocate?

China's giant size is in itself a threat to others, and her smallest aggressive move is regarded with much greater concern than a similar move made by a smaller and weaker country. Like a Gulliver among Lilliputians, China can only avoid hurting others by treading cautiously. If today the Chinese common man must live in privation so that China can arm, it is mainly because the present generation of Chinese leaders have misinterpreted their role and responsibilities in the modern world.

◙   ◙

It has become a favourite pastime in the developing countries to summon conferences at which the sole item on the agenda is the condemnation of imperialism. In view of this and of the fact that one of Chou's major aims in undertaking the tour now under review was to win Africa's consent for one such conference, it is relevant to examine a little more critically who the imperialists are in the world today. Little tangible benefit can emerge from our anti-imperialist activities unless we have a clear idea of whom we are condemning and *whom we should condemn.*

The moribund imperialism of countries like Britain, France and other European powers is well known and loudly criticised in Africa. The United States, whose awesome economic and military power places her in a position to wield the big stick in many parts of the world, comes in for our deserving criticism too. But these traditional and familiar imperialists are not the ones I intend to deal with here. I intend to examine the good faith of three countries—Red China, the Soviet Union and Cuba—which are by far the most vociferous anti-imperialists in the world.

About two years ago, the leaders of the Communist Party of China published an accusation against the Soviet leadership. Part of this reads:

> Contrary to the principles guiding relations among fraternal parties . . . the leaders of the CPSU ignore the independent and equal status of fraternal parties, insist on establishing a kind of feudal patriarchal domination over the international Communist movement, and turn the relations between brother parties into those between a patriarchal father and his sons.
>
> Khrushchev has more than once described a fraternal party as a 'silly boy' and called himself its mother.[7]

This is clearly a charge of neo-colonialism, a form of imperialism. Gheorghe Gheorghiu-Dej, the late ruler of Rumania, had earlier (in 1961) attacked the Soviets for trying to put into practice 'erroneous theories that deny each socialist country the right to build heavy industry' and also of trying to convert Rumania into 'a mere market garden'.

Of course, the Western countries have always accused the Soviet Union of imperialism. But Africa found it convenient to dismiss their word as interideological mud-slinging. Here we have two communist countries accusing a third of imperialism and revealing as a lie their own oft-repeated assertion, that imperialism is incompatible with communism.

Speaking to the Cuban people on February 6, 1966, Fidel Castro launched a blistering attack against the Red Chinese, whom he accused of 'exerting blackmail, extortion, pressure, aggression and strangulation . . . and of the worst methods of piracy, oppression and filibustering'. He further likened China's activities to those of the United States 'when it tried to interfere in [Cuba's] internal affairs and in one way or another impose its will on the nation'. The Soviet Union had, two years before, accused China of warmongering—an imperialist activity. Every time that international relaxation of tension was in sight, the Soviets said, China 'left no stone unturned in order to undermine such a relaxation'. The Soviets then roundly blamed the Sino-Indian border clash on Chinese expansionist (i.e. imperialist) activity.

Even by socialist standards, therefore, China too is imperialist, neo-colonialist, as well as everything else of which Africa accuses her traditional imperialists. By examining Cuba's activities in Latin-America, she too can easily be classed with the other imperialists.

Every time we gather in Algiers or Havana to condemn the imperialists on the same platform with China, the Soviet Union and Cuba, what we really mean is the 'Western imperialists'. But, we might pause to ask, is Western imperialism any more dangerous to us than Eastern imperialism? Our traditional imperialists long ago began a precipitate withdrawal from our continent, leaving only a few strongholds in western and southern Africa for our freedom fighters to demolish. Is it wise, then, to team up now with other and visibly more virulent imperialists who have clearly stated that it is now their turn to expand?

Two enemies, it may be agreed, can profitably pool their energies in a fight against a third and mutual enemy. A good case in point was when Britain, France, the United States and other countries formed an alliance with the Soviet Union to fight their common enemy, Nazi Germany, during the Second World War. The lesson came at the end of the war, when the Soviet Union—alone among the allied countries—emerged as maximum gainer, having stubbornly refused to relax its ideological and economic stranglehold on the East European countries that Soviet armies had liberated.

How can Africa be sure—given the declared expansionist

intentions of the Chinese, Soviet and Cuban imperialists—that, after we have combined with them to overcome the Western imperialists, we ourselves will not in the end be swallowed by those allies?

For a long time to come, we in Africa will still have cause to denounce the imperialists, even if some of us do so merely to draw attention away from our domestic failures. But we need some realism. If any imperialism is dangerous to us, then *all* imperialists are dangerous to us. And if we must have allies, these certainly should not be the confirmed imperialists in Moscow, Peking and Havana. To ally with them can only confirm the opinion they now have of us, that we are *tontos utiles* (useful fools), who act as fronts and lose all in the end, while those who prod them on gain all.

Africa has her own sincere and outspoken men. United we can fight our own anti-imperialist battles.

THREE

Permanent Revolution

Chou En-lai was perfectly right when he said: 'Revolutionary prospects are excellent throughout the African continent.' But there is a difference between his kind of revolution and the kind desired by Africans loyal to Africa. It is noteworthy that Chou carefully reserved this momentous pronouncement to the very last moment of his African tour of 1963–64.

Chou's visit to Somalia had been uneventful until it entered its third day, February 3, 1964. That afternoon, he spoke at a rally held in a stadium in Mogadishu. According to Peter Kumpa's report in the *Baltimore Sun* of February 9, 1964, out of 3,000 or so people present at the rally, half were school-children, and a large number of the people started to stream out even before the speeches began. The poor public address system and the even poorer attempt at simultaneous translation soon caused many more to leave the stadium. There was a near-riot when embarrassed officials frantically tried, with the aid of troops, to keep the crowds in the stadium. Understandably enough, Chinese news reports mentioned nothing of this.

In his 3,000-word address, Chou castigated every imperialist under the sun—all save those of the Chinese People's Republic. He reminded the Somalis of their 'glorious past', in which they played host to 'the Chinese navigator Cheng Ho', trading frankincense and myrrh for Chinese silk. And he made them a gift of his 'Five Principles' with the bonus of his 'Eight Principles' for providing economic aid. The 'revolutionary prospects' piece came somewhere in the middle of the speech.

On the evening of the rally, after a farewell banquet given in his honour by President Osman, the Chinese Premier held a press conference. This lasted until well after midnight. Newsmen fastened on his reference to revolution, and Chou had to explain at length that his interpretation of revolution was quite different from the 'reactionary' meaning which Westerners would read into it. His explanations were not very convincing, particularly in view of the fact that the general subject of Chinese attitudes towards peace and war had cropped up earlier in his tour.

In Tunisia, which Chou visited in early January 1964, President Bourguiba had used the occasion of a banquet in the visitor's honour to criticise China's attempt to spread revolution in Africa, her resort to force in settling frontier problems, and her refusal to sign the test-ban treaty. The *Peking Review*'s report of this part of the tour (No. 3, 1964) mentioned nothing of the Tunisian President's criticisms, but quoted Chou En-lai as saying: 'We can certainly march forward arm-in-arm in the spirit of seeking common ground between us while reserving our differences.' A bland way of replying to censure of one's bellicose and subversive activities!

In the simplest sense, a revolution is a change. It may happen in any sphere of human activity. But in the context we are concerned with, revolution is a matter of politics. Violence in politics may be the first stage in a revolution. The actual revolution begins when, after the supporters of change come to power, they begin to introduce the measures they have earlier proclaimed. Properly speaking, therefore, political revolution means change from an old order to a new. The overthrow of an existing government does not constitute a revolution unless this new order is subsequently established. Thus, when in Latin America one dictator is thrown out and replaced by another dictator, that is no revolution—though it is usually called such by the 'new gang'. Violence is by no means a prerequisite of revolution. Indeed, more revolutions happen peacefully than through violence. We hear more of violent revolutions because, by reason of their dramatic nature, they attract more attention.

During the fifteen years between 1895 and 1910, China had sixteen different uprisings in various parts of the country. But it was only as a result of the sixteenth and more widespread rising in 1911 that the imperial regime was overthrown. Then, after twenty-eight years of almost incessant tumult, the Chiang Kai-shek regime was also overthrown by the communists in a bloody civil war. In consequence of their revolutionary heritage, the Chinese communists find it difficult to accept the possibility of anyone's carrying out a successful socialist revolution without armed force. In an editorial on December 31, 1962, the *People's Daily* argued: 'Hitherto, history has not witnessed a single example of peaceful transition from capitalism to socialism.' If this statement means anything, it is: If you want to turn socialist—the communist kind of 'socialist', at least—start oiling your guns.

In the same editorial, the *People's Daily* roundly attacked Togliatti for his revisionist tendencies. The late leader of the Italian Communist Party believed that it was possible to achieve socialism (even the communist variety) 'progressively', 'peacefully', and through 'a succession of reforms'. The Chinese contended that Togliatti's plea for 'the advance towards socialism in democracy and peace' was reminiscent of the statements of the revisionist Kautsky. And what did Kautsky say: He said: 'I anticipate . . . that it will be possible to carry it [social revolution] out by peaceful, economic, legal and moral means, instead of by physical force.' In other words, through the ballot box, industrial action, legislation and other non-violent means. Since the Chinese disagree with this as violently as they do, it must follow that they stand for revolution by violence, since no middle course exists between 'peaceful means' and 'physical force'.

If you are still not convinced that, by 'revolution', Chou En-lai meant violent revolution, mark this—to celebrate the ninetieth anniversary of the birth of Vladimir Ilyich Lenin, *Hongqi* (Red Flag), the organ of the Chinese Communist Party, stated in its editorial of April 22, 1960: 'Revolution means the use of revolutionary violence by the oppressed class, it means revolutionary war.' Let Premier Chou talk *that* down.

Africa will not soon forget how China held up Algeria as the paragon of revolutionary virtue in this continent. 'The Algerian people', Chou told us, 'have set the African people a brilliant example of daring to wage armed struggle and seize victory, and have designated a correct path for the oppressed nations of the world.' He went on to say: 'We look forward to seeing more Algerias erupt in Africa, just as we are convinced that many more Cubas will appear all over Latin America.'[1] The Algerian people, however, grew weary of being put in the forefront of the revolutionary struggle when their own internal problems cried out for urgent attention. In ousting Ben Bella in June 1965, Boumedienne was able to count on popular revulsion against Ben Bella's demagogic pursuance of the kind of policy Chou commended.

There is a familiar ring about Chou's words. In 1913, Lenin wrote to Maxim Gorky: 'War between Austria and Russia would be very useful to the cause of the revolution in Europe.' Writing about Lenin's activities before 1914, David Shub says of him that 'above all . . . he despised the pacifists . . . who wanted a premature end of the war, thereby destroying the bright prospects of revolution'.[2]

Throughout the history of communism, the story has been the same: war, chaos, revolution—then a communist regime.

And (what sorrow for Africa!), China is not recommending the 'armed struggle' to the still-dependent territories alone, but to 'the African people' as a whole, dependent and independent alike. We must turn 'scientific socialists' in order to please China. And to do it the 'correct' way, we must not choose 'peaceful transition' or legal and moral means; we must start with 'armed struggle', as our self-appointed mentor recommends. As events in the Congo, in Zanzibar and elsewhere amply demonstrate, China and other countries of like aim will make sure that their trained men are on the spot to take advantage of any upheavals that arise as a genuine expression of the people's grievances.

Chou En-lai tried to cajole us into believing that our re-volution cannot be imported, that China is not creating but sup-porting indigenous African revolutions. But here history contradicts him. Revolutions have been exported and imported throughout the ages. When new ideas cross international or other kinds of frontiers, they are exported. By this definition, Marxism was exported from Western into Eastern Europe and Asia; Christianity and Islam were exported from the Middle East into Europe, Africa and other continents; the white man's civilisation was also similarly exported from Europe into Africa and other parts of the world. Before the perfecting of modern media of mass communication, the dissemination of new ideas was painfully slow, and the exporters usually had to travel to the areas which they intended to open up to the new ideas. Today, however, I sit here, receive and am influenced by ideas set down in books and newspapers or broadcast by radio from all over the world.

But new ideas alone, imported or locally generated, do not make a revolution. They must first be accepted and then practised before we can say a revolution has occurred. The forces working against new ideas in general may sometimes be so strong as to make their imposition by force of arms a necessity. Revolutionaries have often found it convenient to import other things than ideas in order to ensure the success of their revolution. Moral and financial support, training facilities, arms and even volunteers may also be exported or granted in aid of a revolution in another country.

We welcome revolutions of many sorts—economic and cultural, for example—but the kind of violent revolution that China preaches, practises and encourages on all possible occasions, is such as to bode little good to any African country that embraces it. Congo is a grim witness.

The powerful nations of the world have always taken advantage of upheavals in the lesser countries to promote their own interests and political systems. Laos, Vietnam, Cuba and Cyprus are examples. In Laos, the flower of the country's youth —the stout arms that should have wielded the hoes to produce more rice, the deft hands that should have tended the machines to manufacture the country's needs—found themselves at the butt-end of rifles and machine-guns bearing the labels 'made in China', 'made in USA', 'made in USSR'. Into battle they marched, armed with foreign weapons—and foreign ideologies. And it was fellow Laotians they slaughtered: not Americans, not Chinese, not Russians.

In Vietnam today, the story is even more bitter. The money that should be spent in building more dams, more schools and more hospitals is instead spent on more rifles and more shells. As the guerrilla campaign intensified, the Vietnamese became what we see them to be today: a people torn by an internal strife which has grown into a major international confrontation between China and America. Men whose talents the country needs to help raise the people from their poverty are killing one another in ambushes and counter-attacks. And in what terms do we reckon the hardship and misery into which this war has plunged hundreds of thousands of widows and orphaned children? All this started as a 'war of liberation'. Is this to be Africa's way to progress?

To the Chinese leaders, violence in preference to peaceful

methods may make sense. The millions slaughtered in their
numerous rebellions, in the civil and foreign wars, and in the
Communist Party's brutal suppression campaigns—these losses
of life have not made any appreciable dent in China's manpower
resources. And I am not at all sure that the Chinese leaders
would not secretly welcome a new war that would eliminate a
few million more hungry mouths without the leadership really
appearing to be responsible for murder.

By contrast, Africa grieves over the millions of her children
who were lost through the slave trade and who died in the
intertribal wars that fed the horrible traffic. In its northern,
eastern, western and central regions, Africa still has great
uninhabited spaces. When these are occupied, we have the vast
wastes of the Sahara and the Kalahari that can in the distant
future be made to bloom and support countless numbers. We
are not yet in such dire need of living space that we should need
to appeal to the bullet. How many can we afford to lose through
senseless mutual slaughter?

I can imagine another reason why China should be interested
in violent revolutions in Africa. One of the points of disagreement between the two communist giants—the Soviet Union
and China—is this: the Soviet Union holds that the socialist
revolution can be carried to other parts of the world by such
'peaceful means' as political and economic subversion. China
maintains that the revolution must be violent in order to
succeed. It is not at all improbable that the Chinese want
Africa to help them win this argument. Stalin himself once
called for an uprising in China (not then communist) to prove
himself right in quarrels with other Bolsheviks. If a number of
violent revolutions should break out on the African continent
and these should be manœuvred in the communists' favour, the
Chinese could then point to us and tell the Russians: We told
you so!

But must we oblige China? Must our children shed their
blood, our resources be squandered in warfare, and all our

past efforts be brought to naught, so that China might win an argument against the Soviet Union?

China may have yet another interest in African revolutions. Pandit Nehru remarked, not long before his death, that African countries were progressing at a faster rate than Asian countries. In a report to the party leadership on March 7, 1957, Madame Li Teh-chuan, Minister for Health in the government of the Chinese People's Republic, said: 'Our country is a big over-populated country. . . . If our population growth is not in accordance with planned childbirth, it will prevent our country from quickly ridding itself of poverty and becoming prosperous and powerful . . . it will inevitably affect the speed of develop-ment of the state industrialisation programme.' China's population in 1953 was 582·6 million; today it is around 700 million, and it is increasing at the rate of about 12 million annually, with the people eating up the agricultural products that should have been sold to obtain capital for industrialisation.

We Africans have an advantage over the Chinese in that few areas in our continent have population problems com-parable to China's. All in all, many of our countries have the makings of rapid advance. Now, if China is to exercise the effective control her leaders desire over the new countries of Africa, Asia and Latin America, it is necessary that she should be some way ahead of them in material development. Yet China's near-insoluble population problem and her con-centration on warlike activities are such a heavy drag on her economic progress that, if the present rates of development were to be maintained in Africa and in China, it would not take very long before a developed (and perhaps also a solidly united) Africa would be in a position to say 'to hell with you' to China. But a warring and permanently divided Africa could not offer any serious challenge to China in the foreseeable future, and so the regime in Peking would have the way clear to establish and maintain its hegemony over us.

◙   ◙

Africa has weaknesses of which not only China but other foreign countries have taken advantage. China was not the only culprit in the Rwanda upheavals (described in Chapter 6). Several influential and 'progressive' African governments were guilty of inciting the Watutsi to war, with the result that when thousands of them were massacred by the Bahutu, not a single African country, apart from tiny Burundi, made a serious protest. Men of conscience all over the world sent fervent appeals for the savagery to end; Africa's contribution was—silence. When white policemen mowed down sixty-nine black Africans in Sharpeville in 1960, all Africa arose and said vehemently what it thought of the accursed apartheid regime down there in the south. But when black Africans massacred several thousands of their fellow black Africans, not even the Organisation of African Unity considered the matter worthy of its serious attention. Does a crime become more heinous, perhaps, if committed by a man of different colour of skin?

In Central Africa, Congo-Brazzaville (the former French Congo) lent itself as a base of operations for terrorists harassing the government of Congo-Leopoldville. The kingdom of Burundi gave shelter to rebels who devastated the Congolese province of Kivu. In both Nkrumah's Ghana and Touré's Guinea, Cameroonian dissidents directing active hostilities in their homeland were given accommodation and funds for their guerrilla operations.

So eager are many of our high politicians to get themselves recognised as 'liberators' that the questions of *whom* they are liberating, from *what* and into *whose* hands, do not seem to be seriously considered by them. All these things still happen, mark you, despite the provisions of Article 2, Principle 2 of the charter of the Organisation of African Unity, which stipulates 'non-interference in the internal affairs of states'.

No less pertinent is the case of little Togo, where a handful of disgruntled soldiers shot down their President in cold blood on January 13, 1963. President Olympio had refused to increase their pay and enlarge the army to absorb ex-servicemen, because he considered the country's purse too slender to afford the luxury of a large army. In the wake of this coup, African foreign ministers ran hither and thither and, finally, condemned *coups d'état* and assassinations as means of changing governments, and also appointed a commission to enquire into the circumstances surrounding Olympio's assassination. But one small man in Togo said 'no enquiry', and, verily, there was no enquiry.

In Zanzibar, a *coup d'état* which was the fulfilment of the legitimate aspirations of a nationalist majority was avidly seized upon by deft hands manipulated by foreign interests. And, what is more alarming, the very men in the Organisation of African Unity who, exactly a year earlier, had publicly condemned *coup d'état* as a political instrument, gave official recognition to the revolutionary regime long before the last rebel gun had sent forth its messenger of death.

What will foreign powers have learnt from our inconsistencies? From Zanzibar they will have learnt that African governments will recognise any new revolutionary regime without pausing to examine what they are recognising, provided only that the nationalist façade is somehow maintained. From Ghana, Guinea, Burundi and Rwanda, they will have learnt that they only need to have approximately identical aims with some power-drunk or power-seeking African leader or politician, in order to hide behind him for subversive purposes. From Togo they will have learnt that any small man whom they back can hold the whole of Africa at bay with the argument: Our internal affair—no meddling.

How excellent, then, our revolutionary prospects!

When Chou En-lai said in Somalia that 'the independent African peoples are building up their respective countries and removing step by step the backwardness and poverty caused by prolonged colonial domination', he was merely taking advantage of the sentimentalism that sometimes blinds our reason in our dealings with the colonialists and ex-colonialists. It is true that the colonialists took away a great deal from our countries. But to say that we derived no benefit from our colonial experience is false. And to say that the colonialists actually *caused* our backwardness and poverty is absurd. Let us examine the case.

At the time my distant forebear met his first white man a hundred and fifty years or so ago, my ancestor's loins might have been girt in cloth made from the bast of some forest tree. He had by that time forgotten how to make the flowing white robes in which his ancestors of ancient Ghana are said to have clothed themselves. When this momentous encounter took place, he might have been on his way to the tiny forest patch that produced the crops for the upkeep of himself and his family. He might háve been holding a small curved machet made by a tribe six miles to the north that had by then learnt how to smelt the iron ore deposits in the hills above their village. Back from his farm he probably took a simple meal of . . . I am not sure what, sparingly seasoned with salt that it took several weeks of trekking to bring from the sea coast not quite 200 miles away; failing sea-salt, he used the powdered bark of some sharp-flavoured root. At night, for fear of prowling beasts, he shut himself in his little hut built of swish and roofed with grass; for light, all he had was his wife's glowing hearth or a flaming torch of dry cane. When ill, he went to the medicine man who gave him a potent herbal remedy or, for a change, a porcupine tail to hang around his neck to ward off evil spirits. His wife probably lost many children within the first few months of birth before any survived. Having no written alphabet, he passed on the tribe's experiences in legends that got all confused with imaginative invention as generation succeeded generation.*

So might my ancestor's life have been before he felt the white

* For the same reason, I admit, I have had to blend some 'imaginative invention' with the scanty facts at my disposal.

man's influence. But the cotton shirt that the white man wore might have awakened in my ancestor a desire to possess something like it. Whether he got the shirt by stealing it, by exchanging an elephant tusk for it, or—eventually—by making it himself, doesn't matter in this argument. What matters is that he had recognised that there were better things than bast cloth. Thus, by his mere presence, the white man had provided a standard for my ancestor to emulate, and it is because my ancestor and his descendants after him found this standard acceptable and did emulate it, that in the place of his reed torch I have a made-in-Africa fluorescent lamp burning above my head now; that in Africa today, instead of being frightened out of our wits, as our ancestors would have been, by those great white birds which noisily ply the skies above us, we travel by them and, what's more, seek to manufacture them in our own countries. We have no cause to be ashamed of having to borrow from another civilisation. Even the civilisers of today were the borrowers of yesterday.

If my ancestor did not feel himself poor or backward, it was because he did not know of any higher standards than those existing in his narrow tribal circle. Today I can say he *was* backward and poor because I have higher standards than he had. A hundred years hence (if American and Soviet—and Chinese—nuclear bombs allow it), my great-great-grandchild may also pity his ancestor of the mid-twentieth century who couldn't even spend a weekend on Mars, just a few million miles away. He, too, will be judging by standards I cannot even imagine now.

Not so long ago, I had the opportunity of seeing how our brothers and sisters live in East and Central Africa. I knew no Kiswahili, no Kikuyu, no Lingala; they knew no Ewe, my mother tongue. But we understood each other wherever I went: we spoke languages imported by the colonialists. African heads of state now regularly meet to discuss matters relating to the unity of Africa. In these conferences not a single one of the

800 local languages and dialects indigenous to Africa is heard. 'Speak English', 'Parlez Français', these are the cries with which delegates have shouted down any North African who has tried to address inter-African conferences in Arabic, for all that it is a language long-established on our continent. If the colonialists 'balkanised' our continent politically, we have at least benefited from their presence, seeing that Africa is now welded into four major linguistic units instead of our original 800. Philanthropy might not have been their aim, but the thing got done. It is now up to us to correct, using the colonialists' languages, the difficulties that arise in Africa in the course of our social, cultural and political evolution.

And, talking of political balkanisation, I have grave doubts about the validity of the argument that the white man balkanised our continent. If I remember aright, this term was popularised in African politics by Kwame Nkrumah. But think of Ghana itself. Before the white man ever set foot there, that area was a heterogeneous collection of tribes having little in common besides their black skins and their backwardness. The most common form of contact between them was intertribal war. Because the white man welded the hundred-and-one tribes into a country with defined boundaries—if not exactly a nation —this Nkrumah was able to gain control over and oppress 7 million people, not just the few tens of thousands of his own tribe. Yet out he trots with 'balkanisation'!

The colonialists committed many sins on this continent. They could have taken away less of our riches or paid better for what they took away; and they could have passed their knowledge on to us faster. But no, they did not *cause* our backwardness.

◻   ◻

The great aim of the Chinese is to cause confusion in Africa or to make the confusion worse confounded where it already exists. Events in East Africa in 1963–64 provided them with yet another opportunity to play on our feelings. In an article captioned "Operation Return", the *Peking Review* (No. 6, 1964) gave a vivid account of how 'the British imperialists never really gave up hope of prolonging their domination', and therefore 'schemed for an opportunity to stage a come-back'. When their chance came in January 1964, 'the British colonialists used brute force to accomplish their "civilising mission" by landing commandos in Dar-es-Salaam after bombardment from the aircraft carrier *Centaur* and the frigate *Rhyl*'. One's blood boils. Yet, when I arrived in Dar-es-Salaam a fortnight after and asked to see the bomb scars, the Tanganyikans thought I was crazy. The plain fact was that, there having been no bombardment, there couldn't have been any bomb scars. But the naval ships did make a great lot of noise; they fired blank shells that told the mutineers in plain and convincing martial language: 'The forces of law and order are awake; beware!' I heard a similar language of the great guns when I arrived in Nairobi on January 27, but to me, as to all peaceable citizens of Kenya, the great guns said: 'Go in peace; the law is behind you.' These are the 'brute force' and the 'bombardment' of which Peking informed the world. And these 'conquerors', the Royal Marines—so perverse were they that instead of shooting down a few thousand Tanganyikans as a very dead example to the rest (as the Chinese themselves would have done at home), they sat on the Dar-es-Salaam seafront blowing *Home, Sweet Home* on their brass instruments. Were they perhaps trying by soft music to hypnotise the Tanganyikans into reaccepting John Bull?

In its articles and broadcasts on these East African events, Peking never once mentioned that the three governments of Tanganyika, Uganda and Kenya voluntarily *invited* the British to help when disorder broke out. Nor could Peking, having started with a lie, report that the three governments publicly thanked the British government for the job its forces had done in helping to maintain law and order. How would it have sounded on Peking's lips—the victim thanking the victor for conquering him! China got no such tribute from the Tibetans.

In Tanganyika, the British 'conquerors' withdrew and were replaced by troops from other African states. In Kenya and Uganda also, British forces were soon withdrawn. Africans might get a little more light from the fact that the Soviet troops who were 'invited' to suppress a revolt in Hungary in 1956 have not yet seen fit to withdraw.

If China would take a leaf out of the book of the British 'conquerors', Tibet could smile again.

◙   ◙

Since all that I have said about China in this and preceding chapters could give the erroneous impression that *all* Chinese are people for ever bent on mischief, I hasten to say that I hold no such view. Quite on the contrary, I have a high opinion of Chinese who do not associate themselves with Peking's aims of world domination and general trouble-rousing.

Like the Red Chinese, the Nationalist Chinese come to our countries to wage a special kind of cold war: they want to make us accept them as the genuine and sole representatives of 'China', and they want to safeguard their position in the United Nations through our support. Much as I deplore cold wars of any kind, I find the Nationalist Chinese in Africa waging their particular cold war in a gentlemanly manner that I cannot help but admire. Without fanfare, their experts come to our countries preaching revolution of a very desirable kind: agricultural revolution. In the countries where their experts work, they have been able to teach local farmers how to raise rice production by as much as 500 per cent on the average. Jute, sugar cane, tobacco and maize are just a few of the numerous food and cash crops that they teach our farmers to grow more efficiently. Thus, by helping our people to eat fuller and more diversified meals and our farmers to increase their earnings, the Nationalist Chinese are helping to fill our hearts with hope in the future and confidence in ourselves: the hope and self-confidence that make indiscriminate bloody revolutions look just what they are—senseless.

Here, at last, we have foreigners who treat us as reasoning adults, conceding to us the right to make our own decisions, and advising only when asked to do so. They come to us with no ideologies, their diplomatists are just what they say they are, and not world revolutionaries on the rampage. African countries that have had to break off relations with Nationalist China, always did so in the special cold war context, and not because of dissatisfaction with Nationalist China's behaviour.

Neither Red China nor Nationalist China ever lays great emphasis on cash when giving aid to our countries. They always emphasise technical expertise, mainly in agriculture and light industries. But, weighed against the good conduct of the Nationalists, is Red China's bad record wherever she steps. It is clear that from Nationalist China, Africa can get most of what Red China can offer, but with the additional advantage that the Nationalists are no danger to our national security. In Africa, the Nationalists really deserve to win.

◙   ◙

I began this chapter by affirming that Chou En-lai was right about the excellence of Africa's revolutionary prospects. But the kind of revolution I have in mind is one aimed at toppling our rather large number of fledgeling dictators. The African commoner in many parts of the continent has come to realise that he was wrong in equating 'independence' with 'freedom'. You don't usher in an era of freedom merely by chasing out the colonial master.

When the colonialists imprisoned our political leaders and agitators, we cried 'oppression'; when they tried to muzzle our press, we cried 'despotism'; and when we thought they sought to make the judiciary serve the will of the colonial executive, we cried 'injustice'. But now that the colonialists have gone, many of our leaders tell us that the best way to make the African learn sense is to imprison him without trial; that a free press is poisonous to the health of society; and that no judgement is just unless it favours the men in power. Because the average African is not an ass, a day will come when he will rise in holy anger and demand the restitution of his free vote, the removal of spies and an end to the forcing of unwelcome foreign doctrines down his throat; a day will come when he will assert the right to identify himself with any political creed or opinion he chooses. These are some of the aims of the kind of revolution I foresee: revolution incontestably 'made in Africa'.*

It is noble and idealistic to talk of changing governments by peaceful and constitutional means. But when *all* these peaceful and constitutional means are denied by the very dictator you need to overthrow, the talk of peaceful means becomes meaningless. Such talk then amounts to acquiescence in our misery and servitude. So I say: if a dictator will not allow his country's government to change hands peacefully, then throw him out, pull him down by *any* means, and to blazes with constitutionality.

But—and I make this a capital BUT—let any such revolution be home-bred, not spawned in China or Russia or America or anywhere else.

* These paragraphs were written before a few more of our dictators were kicked out. We shall certainly be needing similar drastic action to rid us of the rest.

FOUR

The Second Scramble for Africa

Of all the crimes compounded by the Berlin Conference of 1885, the greatest was that the Western imperialists did not consult those whose continent was being carved up in that unholy concert of Europe. After long years, first of passivity and then of active struggle, we have almost completely chased out the Western imperialists from our continent. But now Africa faces another and similar tragedy. The Eastern imperialists have decided in their turn to do a carve-up.

One very important aspect of the Sino-Soviet dispute is how Africa and other underdeveloped countries are going to be converted to the ideology of those Eastern imperialists. Note carefully that their arguments do not concern *whether* we shall be converted, but only *how*—which means that they have decided *for us* that we must be converted. The Russians and the Chinese are at present on divergent paths, and each side is seeking to establish its own camp. The only question which interests them so far as we are concerned is what part of Africa will belong to which communist camp. In all African countries where there are Soviet and Chinese embassies, special local agents are employed to distribute pamphlets and tracts stating their point of view. On the surface, this seems a good thing because it appears to assume that we can, to some extent, reason and judge what is best for us. But here also you detect the parallel assumption that we *have* to go to one or the other side. *Whether* we shall remain positively neutralist, as we have so often and so loudly proclaimed, does not enter into their dispute.

China's Mao Tse-tung—who seems to have the last word for everything—has put it on record that there is no middle way between communism and capitalism. He said, in June 1949 (in his treatise *On the People's Democratic Dictatorship*): 'Sitting on the fence will not do, nor is there a third road.' And he added that 'we also oppose illusions about a third road'. Chairman Mao wouldn't want us Africans to have any illusions either. So here we are between the frying-pan of Soviet communism and the fire of the Chinese kind, and we are warned to look for *no third road*.

When President Nyerere warned of the 'second scramble' for Africa, he said: 'I believe that the socialist countries themselves are now committing the same crimes as were committed by the capitalists before.' It would be a good idea (but what hope is there?) if these self-righteous socialist countries would, with due permission from our governments, hold a referendum to determine whether we want *their* Marxist-Leninist brand of socialism. Mark you, the West is by no means innocent. With an holier-than-thou air, Western countries have arrogated to themselves the sacred duty of protecting Africa from the encroachments of the East's ideological invasion. On all sides everybody assumes that Africans do not know what is right for them. So poor Africa must submit to the indignities of intervention by foreign powers who have little care beyond promoting or protecting their ideological and other interests.

No African would make the claim that our type of socialism —the African socialism which is evolving (and please don't ask me to define it because its very creators haven't been able to define it yet)—is perfect, or even that it *will be* perfect in the foreseeable future. Nkrumah, perpetrator of the most evil practices in the name of African socialism, has been dethroned and discredited. That is more than can be said for any of the Chinese blunderers who were responsible for policies such as the 'great leap forward' which were also carried out in the name of 'scientific socialism'. To me this proves that Africans are capable of evolving a suitable and workable system for themselves.

Under these circumstances, it is not at all heartening to find that some foreign powers propose to replace our not-yet-so-happy blend of socialism and capitalism with another form that is definitely several times worse. Professor Potekhin, the famous Soviet expert on African affairs, said of African socialism early in 1962 that it was being used 'as a means of deceiving the toiling masses in the interest of a capitalist line of development'. The same learned man said in October 1962 that there was no such thing as African socialism, or any other kind of socialism save Marxist-Leninist 'scientific' socialism. 'Scientific' socialism, you should know, is the most direct road to the utopian political system called communism. In 1963, the Lithuanian paper *Kommunist* asserted that the African peoples were moving towards socialism, but added: 'However, there is not and cannot be European, African or any other kind of socialism.' What all this means is that our brand of socialism is not satisfactory to the people out there in the East.

The Chinese put their criticisms much more forcefully. Press reports relate that, while drafting their joint communiqué at the end of Chou's visit to Algeria in 1963, the Chinese and their hosts argued for four whole hours on the question of whether the Algerians were entitled to claim that they were 'building socialism'. In the end, the phrase was dropped. By Chinese standards, then, Ben Bella's Algeria was not socialist; and if it was not, no African country can claim to be 'socialist'.

All our enthusiastic talk about African socialism is just so much nonsense to China and all the others there in the East. What they would like us to practise is *their* brand of socialism: that same brand which, as I have pointed out, is called communism. (I don't know whether it was some ancient imperial Chinese who wrote the first dictionary, but no doubt it is the communists today who want to believe they have the *only* dictionary. I hope our leaders will stick to their guns with 'African socialism' and make of it what *Africans* want it to be.)

In Guinea in the year 1961, the Soviet ambassador, Daniil Solod, was ignominiously expelled from the country. Guinea was then the most socialist of all African countries (Algeria still being at war with France). Due to the fault of de Gaulle, who withdrew aid from Guinea for the 'crime' of voting 'Non' in the 1958 referendum, and of the Americans, who refused aid to Sekou Touré for fear of displeasing de Gaulle (wasted effort when we consider his subsequent boat-rocking in NATO!), Guinea had to turn to the Soviet Union and other Eastern bloc countries. These countries enthusiastically flooded Guinea with various species of experts and technicians, and flattered themselves that they had the country safe in their pocket. But they had reckoned without Sekou Touré; they had reckoned without the African's jealous concern for his new-found freedom. So when comrade Daniil Solod plotted with some French communist teachers to introduce an extremist form of socialism, he found Touré's boot applied squarely to his backside.

On record also is the expulsion of the Soviet and Czechoslovak diplomatic missions from the Congo in 1960. These two countries had between them over 200 diplomatists and technicians in the Congo. The Russians had their own radio transmitter operating from the Congolese capital, Leopoldville (now Kinshasa); there was a Soviet-backed underground organisation responsible for sabotage and infiltration in one of the provinces, and a spy-ring with headquarters in Leopoldville. Many incriminating Russian documents were found in the possession of a prominent

Congolese. The Easterners were preparing to teach the people of the Congo how to be truly and 'scientifically' socialist.

Just as meddlesome are some Western powers who think it their business to prop up regimes that are manifestly unpopular. They do all they can to prevent the overthrow of pro-Western leaders whose removal is not in their interest. Typical examples of this were the Syngman Rhee regime of South Korea, the Batista regime of Cuba, and the Menderes regime of Turkey. These regimes fell as a result of revolutionary pressure, violent or non-violent as the case may be, but there is no guarantee that, the opportunity permitting, the United States and other Western powers will not try the same tricks in some part of Africa.

African socialism has many faults. Indeed, it was an insult even to attach the adjective 'African' to the Nkrumah kind of socialism, because to do so was to imply that the Africans have no regard for the basic freedoms which were taken away from the Ghanaian people in the name of 'African socialism'. And there are practices in other independent African countries which do no credit to the reputation of African socialism. We can— and in order to be strong we *must*—admit this fact.

All the same, it is refreshing to find that the African, faced with opposing pulls from East and West, has at least continued to set a different course and adopt a political system that is neither completely Eastern nor completely Western. The faults of African socialism are for us Africans to correct. We are correcting them. And if, for the time being, we misgovern ourselves in some areas, that is our problem and no one else's. We voluntarily accepted at independence the risk of governing or misgoverning ourselves. That is precisely what autonomy means.

◙   ◙

As if it were not enough for us to have to cope with the conflicting policies in Africa of the two great cold war camps, Western and Eastern, there is the bitter rivalry between the Soviet

Union and the Chinese People's Republic. Both rivals are using the African continent as a main arena for their combat.

Communist China has some 'edge' over the USSR in trying to appeal to Africa, but unless the Chinese leaders can exploit their slight advantage with great skill they are sure to get into trouble. (I should say 'more trouble', for they have made a botched-up job of things in several African countries so far.) China's advantage is that her leaders can point to China's own past as being colonial or 'semi-colonial' and they can say they are non-white (even if they can't say they're black). The big Soviet advantage, to offset this Chinese 'edge', is that the USSR really has made some economic progress and achieved scientific development. The standard of living is still low compared with the rich West, but at least it is vastly higher than in China. So no matter how much the Chinese talk about their 'example', any African who hopes for a rise in living standards is likely to prefer the Soviet example of 'scientific socialism'.

The Chinese leaders, as we can see, are really forced to take the 'revolutionary' stand they take—unless they want to use the good sense to stay at home and build up their own country and mind their own business. If they are not going to do that— if they insist upon 'competing' with the USSR for leadership of the communist bloc and of the Third World—then they have to take the only stand open to them. They have to accuse the USSR of being 'soft' when its leaders talk about peaceful means to achieve the communist end. They have to prate about their 'revolutionary vigour' and brag that they are the only 'pure' Marxist-Leninists on the globe. They have to vow to sacrifice everything for 'permanent revolution'. (If you ask why they have to make this revolutionary stand in *our* continent of Africa, you will be echoing a question many important African leaders also have asked.) In any case, we are promised no sur-cease. Lin Piao, the Chinese Defence Minister who spelled out the plan for an international adaptation of Chairman Mao's guerrilla tactics, also has said that 'it is sheer day-dreaming' to think that the Chinese will 'lose [their] revolutionary fighting will [or] abandon the cause of world revolution'.

The Sino-Soviet rivalry was evident during the African tour of Chou and Chen in 1963–64 even though Chinese and Soviet personnel seldom met in any of the host countries. A visit to the Aswan High Dam project in Egypt, for instance, served to remind Chou not only that the Soviet Union was able to provide aid which China could under no circumstances match, but also that other countries were receiving the kind of help China alienated by her own rash bid to seize leadership from the Soviet Union. (After the collapse of China's 'great leap forward' in 1959, the USSR withdrew almost all technical assistance and material aid the next year.)

In the case of Algeria, the Soviet Union manœuvred to have a 'party-governmental' delegation from Algeria, led by Hadj Ben Alla, visit the Soviet Union at the time Chou was due to go to Algiers. On December 20, 1963, the day of Chou's arrival there, Moscow released Khrushchev's answers to questions from Algerian, Ghanaian and Burmese newspapers. He defended the Soviet record in the support of 'national liberation', and reiterated Moscow's qualifications for the leadership of national liberation movements throughout the world. Soviet coexistence policies, Khrushchev contended, are by no means incompatible with liberation struggles, nor is the support for disarmament a ban on revolution. 'We must expose', he said, 'the harm that is done by replacing the anti-imperialist basis of the solidarity of the peoples fighting for their liberation by geopolitical and even racist ideas.'

All this was clearly aimed at China, even though that country was not specifically mentioned. It summarises very well the basic Soviet policy in the nuclear age: coexistence in cases where Moscow has to face a dangerous Western challenge; encouragement of pro-communist revolutionary movements where international or national opposition is weak; and rebuttal of China's influence.

From Algeria, Chou En-lai fired off his reply to Khrushchev. After declaring that Africans do not need advice from anyone, he proceeded to give us some of his own:

> We do not believe that for Africa the most urgent thing is to fight for disarmament or an abstract thing called 'world detente'. To African leaders and peoples, I try to say that they know better than anyone else what is their most urgent task. Africans know that their most immediate, cherished cause is to fight against imperialism, colonialism and neo-colonialism.

It would seem that everybody knows *our* business and *our* task much better than we do ourselves!

Another good example of squabbling among communists occurred in Mali before and during Chou's visit there. In Bamako, both the Chinese and the Russians were due to hold exhibitions in January 1964. The Mali government had allotted both of them an ample piece of land on the banks of the river Niger. Without prior consultations with the Russians, the Chinese moved in to stake out the centre of the entire site, and began erecting their exhibition building on it, thus forcing the Russians to move to a less favourable site. The Chinese irritated their 'socialist brothers' even further by displaying all their documents relating to the Sino-Soviet ideological dispute. As a counter-blow, the Russians hired hundreds of Malian youth to distribute pamphlets in the streets and to the crowds waiting at the airport to welcome Chou En-lai on January 16. The pamphlets stressed in detail the Soviet Union's aid and achievements in Africa, contrasting these with the insignificant contribution of China.

Similar scenes of Sino-Soviet rivalry were enacted in Guinea, Ghana and Somalia. And Chou carried the argument over to Albania with him when he broke his African journey at the New Year holiday to visit 'fraternal Albania' and its leaders.

Plate 1a   Chou in Guinea, January 16–21, 1964

Plate 1b   Chou in Accra, January 11–15, 1964; with
President Nkrumah at presidential residence

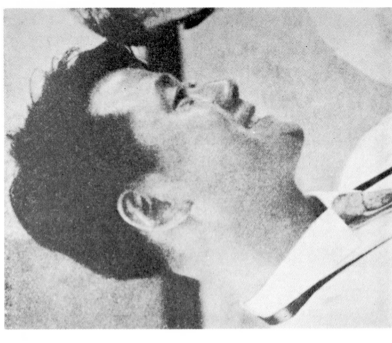

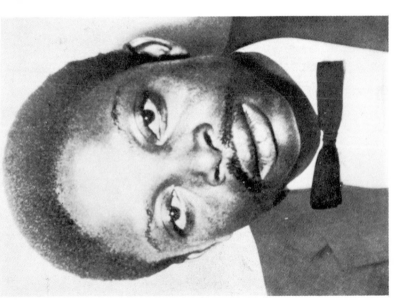

Plate 2a Pierre Mulele, leader of revolt in Kwilu Province, Congo

Plate 2b Kao Liang, NCNA correspondent and Chinese agent in Zanzibar and Burundi

Plate 3a Guerrilla Training Camp, Obenemasi, Ghana: Lt Yang Te-yeh, and St Capt Li Fu-kun, explosives expert, lecturing on explosives

Plate 3b Guerrilla Training Camp, Obenemasi, Ghana: Lt Yang Te-yeh, and St Capt Li Fu-kun teaching class how to handle dangerous explosives

Plates 4a and b   Women in Training

Albania is a mountainous little strip of a country lying along the Adriatic coast. Its total population is less than 2 million persons. In other words, any one of several Chinese cities is much larger than Albania; it has about half as many people as Cairo has. There is nothing wrong about being a small country; I mention some facts about Albania only because the Chinese leaders talk so much about Albania that one might get the idea it is a world power. Small as it is, however, Albania is giant China's good friend; in fact Albania often seems to be China's *only* friend. And what Albania lacks in size and population she makes up for in fierceness. No one is more revolutionary. Thus Albania was the perfect platform from which Chou En-lai, breaking his African tour, could relieve himself of the pronouncements which would not go over at all well on the African continent.

Chou spoke out plainly, and so did his hosts. The Sino-Albanian joint communiqué, which the *Peking Review* described as 'a historic document', included the following passages:

Both China and Albania are determined to strengthen further friendship and unity between the two parties and countries. . . . Both agree that the present international situation continues to develop in a direction favourable to the revolutionary people of the whole world. . . .

Both denounce the American-British-Russian partial nuclear test-ban treaty . . . and reaffirm that [they] always stand for general disarmament and for the complete prohibition and thorough destruction of nuclear weapons.

Both pay warm tribute to and resolutely support the struggles of the peoples of Asia, Africa and Latin America against imperialism. . . . Both firmly support the mass struggles waged by the working class and other labouring people of the capitalist countries. . . .

The Chinese government and people strongly denounce the imperialists, reactionaries of all countries and modern revisionists for all their intrigues to isolate and injure

Albania. . . . Both [countries] hold that it is now the sacred
duty of the Communists of all countries to combat modern
revisionism and modern dogmatism.[1]

Chou En-lai, during the Albanian visit, hurled particularly
abusive remarks at Yugoslavia, Albania's neighbour and her
opposite in the Sino-Soviet feud. In fact, during the early days
of Sino-Soviet rivalry, Albania and Yugoslavia served as
'stand-ins' for the real opponents. Neither side, in those earlier
days, mentioned each other. China's leaders spoke of the 'Tito
revisionists' when they actually meant the USSR, and Soviet
spokesmen criticised Albania when they really meant China.
Eventually the altercation became so obvious to everyone in
the world that the substitution of names was ludicrous.

According to the Belgrade newspaper *Politika*, Chou En-lai's
speech in Scutari, Albania, was a vitriolic attack on Marshal
Tito of Yugoslavia. That speech, the paper reported, contained
such endearing phrases as 'the renegade Tito's clique . . . will
be liquidated once and for all' and 'we will break their heads'.
But right after Albania, Chou went to Tunisia where the chant
from his honeyed tongue was again 'peaceful coexistence'.
Africa has the right to ask: China, where do you stand? Are
you coexisting with others or just co-breaking heads?

It is alarming to note how internal conflicts among communists determine their policy towards us peoples in the underdeveloped world. Not that there is anything new in this. Just
as the early Comintern policy toward China and the East, as
W. A. C. Adie points out, was governed by Stalin's conflict
with Trotsky, so is Peking's policy towards Africa governed
by its conflict with Moscow. Between 1949 and 1955, Peking's
policy was more or less the same as Moscow's. Then, in the
post-Bandung period and up to 1959, strong indications
appeared of China's preparing herself to rival Russia. The third
stage in Peking's policy dates from 1959 and is governed by the
open hostility between the two great communist states.

Much of Peking's activity in Africa is simply meant to muster Africans as extras for a sort of super-colossal Peking opera, full of sound and fury, in which Mao Tse-tung fights his Chinese battles all over again on the world-wide stage: just to prove that China, not Russia, 'shakes the world' and deserves proper respect.[2]

Both sides of the Sino-Soviet dispute showed an early interest in the 'revolutionary situation' in Africa by trying to exploit Pan-Africanist feelings and movements. When African heads of state were meeting at Addis Ababa in May 1963 to draw up the Charter of African Unity, messages were received from Khrushchev and Chou En-lai. Both sides made great play of the contribution the conference could make in the fight against neo-colonialism. Chou's message set out to stress the necessity of solidarity with the Asian world, while Khrushchev sought to align Africa on the Soviet Union's side in the 'world anti-imperialist, anti-colonialist front'.

In fact, the conference affirmed a policy of non-alignment in world affairs, which was a rejection of communist aims. But since then, scenting the 'revolutionary prospects', both Russia and China have continued to pursue the same tactics. China has tried to draw all African bodies into 'Afro-Asian' organisations, while Russia has tried, by voicing support for African aspirations, to line the continent alongside her against the West on every possible occasion. The USSR also has made a concerted effort to be accepted into Afro-Asian groups (citing the fact that much of her territory lies in Asia), and China has made an even greater effort to keep the Soviet Union *out*. The whole issue of actual Afro-Asian interests and unity, I might add, has been submerged in this Sino-Soviet fight.

At the third conference of the Afro-Asian Peoples' Solidarity Organisation, held at Moshi in February 1963, the Chinese delegation went around saying: 'We coloureds must stick together.' The Soviet delegation complained that the Chinese made 'openly racialist attacks' on them, asserting that they (the Russians) 'are whites; it is impossible to agree with them in the struggle against imperialism'. The *Daily Nation* (Kenya), commenting on this AAPSO meeting said:

> In the hotels of Moshi and in the committee rooms of the conference, the Chinese are pouring out the unceasing message: the Russians are going to let you down. Look at Cuba, look at the agreements on coexistence between Khrushchev and Kennedy. It is all clear indication that, as Whites, the Russians are going to back the Whites. But we are Coloureds and your blood brothers in the struggle. Only we can understand your problems.

It was at this conference that President Nyerere noted the existence of a 'second scramble for Africa' between Russia and China for staking out political spheres of influence. Wherever possible, China tries to counter Russian influence. A Chinese gift of £1 million and a loan of £5·3 million were made to Kenya in May 1964, three days after the Russians had promised a hospital and a technical school as gifts. In June of the same year, China ousted Russia as the main communist donor to Tanzania, offering loans worth £16 million. The loans were interest-free, but were conditional on China's providing technical assistance. Aid of this kind is certainly useful to us in Africa, even if it falls short of our needs and is on a much smaller scale than that received from Western countries. But what is not so useful is the foothold it may give China, if our leaders are not careful, for carrying forward its policies of subversion and domination.

What worries me is that, in their mutual rivalry, the Chinese and Russians are seeking to outbid one another, not only in offers of aid, but in political manœuvres to gain influence over our countries. And conflicts between the two communist powers could lead to conflicts between African countries. The Sino-Soviet dispute for Africa is both a bore and a menace. The meeting of the Afro-Asian Peoples' Solidarity Organisation in Algiers in March 1964 was completely disrupted by the mutual slanderings of the Soviet and Chinese delegations. A Kenyan representative complained:

> We are not Marxists-Leninists. Most of us have not read a line of *Das Kapital*, so what interest do you expect us to show in your doctrinal quarrels? I am tired of being asked what I think of the Soviet position when I am eating a sandwich, and what I think of the Chinese arguments when I am drinking my tea.

The proposed 'Second Bandung' in 1965 presented Africa and Asia with another example of how China and the Soviet Union seek to manipulate us for their own ends. Because the Chinese wanted to play the leading role in this conference, even as they did at the original Bandung meeting, they found it necessary to try to exclude the Soviet Union by deploying the racial argument: 'You are not of our Afro-Asian group; you are white.' The Russians, of course, countered by pointing out that by far the larger part of their national territory lies within Asia. Further moves by China to exclude Israel, South Vietnam and other countries from participation left no room for doubt that an Afro-Asian country, by Chinese definition, is one that is exclusively friendly with China or China's friends.

Ben Bella, at the time he held sway in Algeria, was Chou En-lai's closest friend and confidant in Africa. But the moment he fell from power, the Chinese government recognised Houari Boumedienne with indecent alacrity lest it miss the chance of standing to the fore on the rostrum of the Afro-Asian conference planned to take place in Algiers. What, then, must have been the surprise of African leaders when they saw that the very man who sold his 'Algerian brother' down the river in July to make sure the conference was held, by November was sparing no efforts to have the rescheduled conference cancelled?

The fact was that, by November 1965, China was swimming in scalding waters. Her diplomats had been expelled from Burundi, Kenya and Dahomey for subversive activities, and severely censured in other African countries for the same offence. Her attempt to aggravate the Indo-Pakistani conflict had revealed her clearly as an incorrigible warmonger. China's part in the abortive coup of September 30, 1965 in Indonesia had smeared her darker with the stain of faithlessness towards professed friends. China, then, rather than the Western powers, would probably have been the target of vehement attack and condemnation had an Afro-Asian conference been held at the end of 1965. That China torpedoed this conference shows that it was her own ambitious interests, and never ours, that were motivating her exertions in convening it in the first place. But what must sadden us most of all is that many African leaders, whom their people trusted to judge wisely in Africa's interests, supported China in these cynical political somersaults.

Perhaps the most sickening aspect of the communist attempt —both Russian and Chinese—to exploit Pan-Africanist feelings is the blatancy of their lip-service to our demands for justice for our fellow Africans in South Africa. Peking and Moscow, to go by their words, are zealous for the prosecution of the severest economic boycott against South Africa. Yet, while African countries have suffered a good deal of hardship by implementing the boycott, Soviet craft have flouted the embargo on the Apartheid Republic's ports and airfields, and China and the East European countries have been steadily increasing their trade with it.

This cynical double-faced attitude over South Africa was shown up by the communists themselves in their wranglings with one another. At about the time of Chou's tour of Africa, the Russians passed the word round in various African capitals that the Chinese still maintained trade relations with South Africa (not mentioning, of course, Russia's own disregard of the embargo). These charges the Chinese vigorously denied.

But the Afrikaner newspaper *Die Burger*—which, if it is going to propagandise, will certainly not do so for Black Africa—reported in August 1963 that China's imports from South Africa in the first quarter of 1963 rose to Rand 3·7 million (£1,850,000). Confirmation of this rate of trade came a month later in the Cape Town *Sunday Times*:

> Trade with Communist China is continually increasing. South Africa exported Rand 4,227,431 [more than £2 million] worth of goods in the first four months of this year, During the same period last year there was virtually no trade with China. South Africa imported Rand 1,064,478 worth of goods this year as compared with Rand 190,457 last year.[4]

In June 1964, the Chinese repeated their denial of any trade between them and South Africa, and called reports of such trade 'lies'. But the *China Mail* of Hong Kong observed:

> Figures for the first six months of 1964 are not yet available, but there are indications that the trade has continued, with Peking either making purchases directly from South Africa or indirectly through commercial brokers.[5]

When L. M. Barett, chairman of the South African Chamber of Commerce, was asked by a Hong Kong journalist whether South Africa's apartheid policy was an obstacle to trade with China, he replied: 'None whatever.' South Africa has a permanent trade commissioner stationed in Hong Kong to deal with trade between the Apartheid Republic and Mao's regime.

Peking has good reasons to denounce all this as lies put out by the West or the Soviets. In fact, most of the censure of this trade between South Africa and China has come from Soviet sources: 'A thief crying "grab the thief" ', as an old Chinese saying puts it. But there is an ominous significance for us in the statement made by *Borba*, the Yugoslav official paper, on July 20, 1964: 'This trade is being intensively continued and, according to a UN report on international trade, China also

supplies South Africa with explosives.' The Kenyan Minister for
Commerce and Industry, Dr Kiano, also commented on this
situation.

> I can cite a good number of South African companies and
> financial institutions which are known in the international
> trade circles to be vehicles for carrying out and financing
> trade between South Africa and China. . . . International
> trade is very difficult to conceal, and if the government of
> China is unable to discover the channels through which that
> trade is still going on, I for one am willing to come to her aid
> and provide the necessary guideposts for that government.[6]

Many countries have refused to co-operate in the trade boycott
against South Africa, and have clearly declared their intention
of maintaining economic links with that country. If this doesn't
help us, at least it is frank and we know where we are. But to
blare forth from the rooftops and go around protesting the
strongest support for Pan-Africanism, as China and Russia do,
and then continue economic relations 'on the side'—this is
something more than hypocrisy: it is a cynical insult to us
Africans. The Kenya *Sunday Post* commented justly:

> It must be disappointing to OAU leaders who are pressing for
> sacrifices by opponents of the South African system to see
> that, while Britain, often accused of undercover support for
> apartheid, is prepared to forego orders worth £150 million,
> recent statistics reveal that by far the biggest increase in
> trade with the Republic over the last few months has been
> with some of the most vociferous advocates of the exertion
> of economic pressure to bring South Africa to heel.

Such are the Simon Pures who are urging *us* to revolutionary
sacrifices!

Chou En-lai likes to tell us to rely on our own efforts. Why,
I wonder, does he not encourage us therefore to rely on our
own efforts to evolve our own form of socialism, suitable to

African conditions and aspirations? We could, I am sure, turn out a 'backyard socialism' that would be more useful than the poor Chinese people's 'backyard steel' was in 1958.

The best way in which any non-African power can show true political friendship towards Africa is to leave us alone to explore, experiment and finally adopt a system most suited to our conditions. We are not impressed by loud professions of friendship that serve only to mask the intention to make us pawns in an international power game while carving out spheres of influence among us.

FIVE

Revolutionary Situations: I

A revolutionary situation may be said to exist in a country when a section of the population is dissatisfied with its conditions, seeks to change them and believes the existing political, social or economic system cannot effect the change. Generally, the larger the section affected, the more explosive the situation. When, for example, a large number of Africans became dissatisfied with their colonial status and began to struggle for independence, a revolutionary situation of great magnitude came into being. The recognition by a people that they are backward in comparison with another people, and the consequent desire to move forward from backwardness, also constitute a revolutionary situation. Even dissatisfaction with wages can be a revolutionary situation, depending on the extent of the dissatisfaction and on whether the workers or other interested bodies have a plan to exploit the situation for other ends. 'If we have a strongly organised party,' wrote Lenin in the first issue of *Iskra* in December 1900, 'a single strike may grow into a political demonstration, into a political victory over the regime.'[1] The kind of strike Lenin advocates here is one that, without necessarily being overtly political to begin with, may be manipulated by a political group whose ultimate aims may be quite different from those of the strikers.

By the above analysis, Africa is at present in the throes of several full-scale revolutions—political, social and economic— albeit of kinds that need neither be violent nor precipitate. I intend to survey briefly such of our revolutionary situations as can be manipulated into violent revolutions as Lenin recommends. Our revolutionary situations are of two broad categories:

1. Situations calling for revolt against oppression by colonialist regimes;

2. Internal strains and stresses favouring upheavals in independent African states.

REVOLT AGAINST COLONIALIST OPPRESSION

Conditions existing in those parts of Africa where a white minority still dominates a black majority are certain to be among the continent's most explosive revolutionary situations: first, because Africans within these colonial enclaves are either preparing for or are already engaged in armed revolt; secondly, because many independent African countries are eager to lend their support; and thirdly, because of the potentialities for intervention by outside powers.

Those colonial powers which have been forced to recognise the black African's right to rule himself have already granted, or affirmed their intention to grant, independence to their colonies. In the case of the British in West Africa, the colonial power not only granted independence but endeavoured to give its colonies a reasonable measure of preparation for self-government.

But Portugal still follows the policy of 'education for servitude', which, as practised by Belgium, contributed so much to the Congo's instability after independence. The 'wind of change', which has amply demonstrated to other Western

countries that they cannot hold their colonies indefinitely, has
still to blow in Lisbon. In view of the intransigence of the
Portuguese over the question of independence for their colonies,
it appears that a new method of struggle becomes necessary,
and that the peaceful methods used in most African countries
cannot easily be applied in 'Portuguese' Guinea, Angola,
Mozambique and the rest. The alternative is obviously the
armed revolt in which several of the Portuguese colonies are
now engaged. But their experience to date has shown that,
desirable as it may be, such armed struggle is not to be engaged
in without serious forethought.

For the five years since March 1962, the Angolan nationalists
have been fighting an anti-colonial war that shows little prospect
of ending in our favour. Hundreds of thousands of non-
combatants have been uprooted from their homes and have
had to flee into exile in surrounding countries. Repressive
counter-measures by the Portuguese armed forces have made
life unbearable for countless numbers who could not flee the
territory. Because aid from the independent African states has
been fitful and inadequate, the suffering and misery caused by
the war are likely to continue for some time yet.

The little war in 'Portuguese' Guinea has similarly dragged
on for four years without victory coming in sight. On the whole
our conduct of these anti-colonial wars has been so half-hearted
that all Africa is now held in contempt by the colonialists—
even by tiny Portugal. In view of this, I see little sense in
issuing further threats that have little chance of being followed
by vigorous armed action. What I believe we can and should
do is to concentrate on one or two of these territories and fight
with all the energy and resources we can muster. If we can win
a decisive victory in just one territory, we shall have proved
that we have both the sound teeth that can bite and the courage
and unity to face the enemy. It is only when we have proved
this that Portugal and Southern Africa can respect our threats
of armed action. The longer these wars last, the greater the

temptation to seek military aid from countries ready to wriggle themselves into our favour for their own purposes.

It is believed in some Portuguese official circles that, if only the United States would exert a little pressure on certain African states, the revolts in Angola, Guinea and Mozambique could be suppressed once and for all. But such pressure would be a great disillusionment to many, both inside and outside the United States. It would be a slap in the face to American liberal opinion which, with the heightening of the Civil Rights campaign, is now in the ascendant; and it would be such an insult to the whole of Africa as would damage America's image in our continent beyond repair. If I might presume to teach the Americans a bit of their own business, I would say that they should not be obsessed by their economic interests, or give too much weight to Portugal's utility to their military interests as a NATO member and as lessor of the United States military base in the Azores. They should consider what is fair and just by their own best lights. They should act in the spirit of the preamble to their Declaration of Independence: 'We hold these truths to be self-evident', it runs, 'that all men are created equal, that they are endowed by their creator with certain inalienable rights, that among these are life, liberty and the pursuit of happiness . . . Governments are instituted among men, deriving their powers from the consent of the governed.'

Since the people of Angola, Mozambique and the other Portuguese colonies are among the 'all men', the Portuguese, with whom they are 'created equal', have absolutely no right to assume superior powers over them, particularly since the Africans have made it quite clear that such overlordship is now intolerable. Portugal's power in Africa no longer derives—if it ever did—from the 'consent of the governed'. The arguments that were good enough for driving the British out of the thirteen American colonies are good enough for throwing the Portuguese and any other colonial masters out of Africa. The Americans conceive it their duty to defend freedom in Vietnam, Laos and

Latin America; but Africa cannot accept their good faith unless they also exert the maximum possible pressure on Portugal and on other colonialist regimes in the name of African liberty.

I would therefore reverse the conclusions drawn by the Portuguese, and say: If only the United States and their NATO allies would put pressure on Portugal; if only they would stop supplying arms and funds to Portugal, either openly or covertly; if only they would make it plain in their acts, not just in words, that they are rootedly opposed to Salazar's policies—then the war in the Portuguese colonies would end in a short time, and the peoples of these colonies would win the right to govern, or misgovern, themselves. This argument applies with equal force to the situation in Southern Africa.

We welcome dollars for dams and Peace Corps for our schools. But what Africa demands above all is positive support in our fight against the remaining colonialists, and in our struggle to win dignity and respect for ourselves and for our fellow-Africans in Portugal's empire, in Rhodesia and in South Africa. The United States and the European powers must choose between Africa and Salazar, between Africa and Ian Smith, between Africa and Vorster. They must choose in the name of the ideals they profess—and also in their own interests, for the revolutionary situation in these colonialist regimes, if it continues, will explode into the kind of conflagration which revolutionaries of the Peking-type will seek to make the death-pyre of the West.

In the independent countries of East Africa, a measure of concord has been achieved between the races, and it is to be hoped that nothing will happen in future to mar this encouraging example of racial harmony. It is disheartening, indeed, that the white settlers in Rhodesia have not found the example worthy of emulation.

But I cannot be blind to the fact that, though the policy of the white Rhodesian government is detestable, not everything in their case is to be dismissed utterly. The Rhodesian whites, like all settlers on our continent (and, if we think of it a bit, are not a good many of us Africans settlers too? Can we swear that our forebears were always where we are now?) might have been less intransigently opposed to rule by a black majority if we had given them better grounds for confidence in such rule.

By dint of toil and patience, the white Rhodesians have created for themselves an economy and a standard of living that ranks among the highest in the world. But now they observe that the first thing most of our African rulers do is to put the economy in a thorough-going mess. What is to happen to the standards they have established for themselves, they ask, if a black government in their country were to follow that deplorable precedent?

Mostly of British stock, white Rhodesians are attached to a freedom-loving tradition. (Freedom for themselves, that is.) But now they see that African countries in which people shout 'freedom!' loudest are precisely those in which that desirable commodity is scarcest. They have seen black rulers oppress and push their brother blacks around. They have some right to ask themselves: if the black man can do such things to his kith and kin, then what will happen to *us* under rule by a black majority? And, what is more, many of those who are foremost in the attack on the white Rhodesians are the very men who, by oppressing their own compatriots, have done the most to undermine confidence in government by black Africans. They talk bravely of shooting the white man into submission in Southern Africa. But what of the other approach: making black government synonymous with justice, freedom and peaceful progress— with a form of rule in which white and black, majority and minority, can have confidence?

In the Republic of South Africa, we meet with a peculiar subspecies of white man: the Boer. He is the least reasonable of the white race. He is a man to whom the theory and practical effects of biology are so alien that, though he may admit, if educated, that skin colour has no direct correlation with intelligence, he vigorously asserts the precise contrary in legislation and social behaviour. What I recognise in the Boer are two things: a bitterness of mind and heart so deep-rooted as to make him incapable of reason and humane feeling on racial issues; and a tormenting fear. The Boer's apartheid is the child of racial prejudice and fear. And his fear is more to be feared than his racialism.

The noblest minds of South Africa, and the most respected men in Africa and all over the world, have joined their voices to condemn the injustice and vileness of apartheid. The Boer, and those South Africans of British origin who throw in their lot with the apartheid policy, remain unconvinced and unmoved. Strikes, boycotts, demonstrations and resolutions— Africa has gone through the gamut. And what have we won for our pains? Sharpeville; the persecution of African leaders; more and more repressive laws.

Sometimes a man just has to stand and fight. South Africa is the place where Africans will have to do just that, regardless of the dangers involved.

But, as I have said before, we still need to prove—and soon— that we can stand and fight.

And even this war, when we finally come round to fighting it, must be a war in defence of justice and human dignity, not just a war against the white man down south. We cannot afford to fight a race war. In a race war, even in victory, we shall be the losers. If a section of the white race oppresses us, by far the greater section brings the bulk of the money and the know-how that build the big dams.

INTERNAL STRESSES

1. *Unfulfilled Hopes*. With eloquence born of the inviting prospect of a ministerial post or a parliamentary seat, our politicians blamed on the colonialists every evil in our pre-independence society. We logically expected that with the colonialists out of the way, our lot would be much happier. Such hopes were

strengthened in some countries by the politicians positively and unwisely promising us the same villas, the same long cars and princely life we used to associate with the white master in colonial Africa. But when independence came and nothing changed except that the politicians had neatly stepped into the former white masters' shoes, the masses became, first confused, then angry. Their anger rose to boiling point when short-sighted and unrealistic economic policies scared away prospective investors and led to increased unemployment. In many countries, much money was spent on projects that had little relevance to the people's actual needs. The cost of living rose, and the economic hardships, coupled with the denial of the basic human freedoms, have already led to explosions in some countries, with many more on the verge of collapse for the same reasons.

But I must say, in fairness to these petty dictators, that we the masses helped a great deal in creating them. If we had been less gullible, they would not have fed us with so many lies; if we had been less sycophantic, they would not have got the impression that they could get their way any time they chose; and if we had shown in our actions that we did have values we were prepared to defend, they would have been less inclined to assume the role of sole and absolute guiding lights.

In short, we the masses have been too spineless in the past. We were oppressed because we proved to be fit subjects for oppression.

2. *Interethnic conflicts.* Interethnic conflicts are also ready-made revolutionary situations. We may recall the case of the Sudan where, for ten years and more, the Sudanese of Negro stock have been in constant armed revolt against Arab Sudanese, whom they accuse of adopting a 'crude policy of suppression and assimilation of the African south into the Arab pattern of life'. In the field of education, the government is accused of carrying out its arabisation policy by replacing the Christian missionary schools with its own schools and

substituting Arabic for the local languages in which the missionaries formerly instructed the people. Over 400 foreign missionaries are said to have so far been expelled because, as the government argues, they had ceased to be useful to the country after the schools were taken over from them. Some of these missionaries were also alleged (I am not clear with what justice) to have had partial responsibility for the unrest in the south.

In Rwanda and Burundi similar tensions exist between the Watutsi and the Bahutu, and have already led to bloody armed clashes. As we shall see in the next chapter, these tensions have been extensively exploited by outside forces seeking to gain a foothold in the area.

Former Belgian Congo's age-old tribal feuds have provided fertile ground for both indigenous revolutionaries and international trouble-rousers. Twice within the five years beginning from 1960, Africa has had reason to fear that the Congo might turn into another Vietnam, where the world powers, afraid to fight a nuclear war, confront each other in a 'safe' ideological war on somebody else's soil. A little probing shows that irreconcilable tribal loyalties and enmities were deciding factors in the two major Congolese upheavals.

In Nigeria, as in Chad, Kenya, Uganda, Ivory Coast and many other African countries, interethnic quarrels have created revolutionary situations aggravated in some places by political parties being tribally aligned. In such cases it only requires one side to receive some sort of aid or encouragement from one world power for the other side to ask for aid from an opposing power. Explosions have so far been avoided in many of these interethnic tensions, but they remain a stand-by for intending revolutionaries.

3. *Racialism*. Elsewhere in this chapter, we have seen that the black and white races in Africa are heading for a collision that can only be averted if reason prevails on both sides. As I have pointed out, if moral arguments have so far had little effect on the white settlers down south, it is because we Africans

concentrated more on precept than on example. What is more, we have used these moral arguments in the wrong way altogether. Our case would have been immeasurably strengthened in world opinion if we had condemned the white settler solely in the name of justice and fair play. But in a continent where we have been witnessing the at once sad and ridiculous spectacle of a ruler denying the vote to his countrymen and yet levying a militia to defend the free vote 2,000 miles away in Rhodesia, arguments based on these virtues are so hollow that we are reduced to using purely racial arguments—practising towards the white settler the very opposite of what we so sanctimoniously preach to him. If black Africans will defend other black Africans in Southern Africa merely because of their identity of colour and race, what prevents the white man in Britain or Australia or Canada from defending his white cousins in Southern Africa for precisely the same reason? Thus do we, with our racial arguments, alienate the sympathy of millions all over the world, who would otherwise have been our supporters.

In many of our countries where there is a mixture of races, racial hatred has indeed been buried, but in such a shallow grave that the slightest scratch reveals the whole stinking mess once again. I will cite just one example.

In Tanganyika, Dr Julius Nyerere started a hopeful experiment that has since been copied by both Kenya and Uganda. In Kenya they call it *Harambee*: the spirit of co-operation in which black, brown, and white alike will move hand in hand, in peace and concord and towards progress. Here, at last, was Africa's hope: an argument which might make the white Southern African pause and ponder; an argument which says plainly: *Even when he is in the majority, the black African can be reasonable towards the other races*. Then, that sad day came when some soldiers in Tanganyika took it into their heads to mutiny for higher pay and for the withdrawal of British officers from the army. This mutiny provided an excuse for the black population of Dar-es-Salaam to persecute their fellow-citizens of other colours, the Asians particularly, and the future of this grand experiment in East Africa became clouded in doubt. The reason for the revival of this race feeling was that the Asians, who have for a long time occupied a position of privilege next to the white settlers, became identified with the exploiter class by reason of their vast commercial interests in the area.

But, with goodwill, what fell can be rebuilt. My fear is that those in whose interest it is to create violent revolutions, and those in whose interest it is that Africa should remain backward, may tickle us on this racist soft spot and incite us to destroy, where we need to build.

4. *Refugees and Political Exiles.* The life of a political exile is one of constant plotting and scheming. I say this as one who has been an exile. It is almost impossible to resign oneself to a life of uncertainties and of indefinite separation from loved ones at home. So, whatever might have led to a political exile's flight from his homeland, he will plot his return, no matter what regulations his country of refuge may have against such activity. He sees himself fighting in a holy cause, with the mission of restoring to himself and his countrymen the rights he feels are denied. For men with such revolutionary fervour, almost any method is good enough if it promises success. What makes such exiles more dangerous as revolutionaries is that, in their desperation, they are prepared to accept help even from the devil himself.

Obviously, the one way to avoid violent revolutions planned by exiles is to remove all the conditions that create exiles. If political opponents can say their piece without fear of being hauled to jail without trial, there will be little need for anyone to want to speak or plot from abroad. If our judiciaries are no longer tied to the rulers' apron-strings, a man accused of a political offence need not automatically feel a condemned man. Instead of fleeing abroad at the first hint that he is suspected, he will more likely stay and face trial by judges whom he has learnt to trust.

In Africa, as elsewhere, oppression breeds resistance, which, in turn, breeds the kind of violent revolutions we should avoid. If African leaders will start ruling *for the people* instead of *against the people*, they will have set our countries on a course that makes violent revolutions as undesirable as they will be unnecessary.

5. *Cold War*. The East-West cold war and the Sino-Soviet dispute are not African revolutionary situations in themselves, but they affect us so profoundly that this chapter would be incomplete without considering this subject.

When an African dictator suppresses opposition at home to the point where his opponents see no other way out than armed force, the first thing they think of is where the funds are to come from for the implementation of their plans. The existence of cold war camps makes the choice very easy indeed. If the dictator leans towards the communist camp, his opponents seek help from the West, and vice versa. The hope of establishing some influence makes the world's cold war factions jump at the opportunity of aiding dissidents. Without the availability of such help, most of our revolutionary plans would be stillborn for lack of means to carry them out.

Sometimes, also, a tolerably fair and just government (by African standards) is assailed by revolutionary forces trained and financed from abroad, just because some power outside does not like the government's ideological complexion.

There is no country with a government so good that it has no dissenters. Indeed, dissent is an essential of good government. It is only when our dissenters are recognised and treated as normal citizens who happen to think differently that they can be wooed away from thoughts of revolution as a political instrument. Added to such change of heart at home, our governments can try to be so genuinely and nicely non-aligned that foreign powers will not consider it in their best interest to disturb the delicate balance.

In this chapter as well as in the previous one I have spoken strongly about what I consider to be some of the more flagrant inconsistencies and weaknesses in African political life.

Many ex-colonial powers have pointed at these inconsistencies and at our dictators as proof positive of our inability to govern ourselves. How short their memory! If dictatorship alone is a sign of political backwardness and immaturity, then I can conceive few people so unripe for self-rule as the Germans of the thirties, who tolerated a God-forsaken and God-forsaking man like Adolf Hitler. I fail to see why the Russians should consider themselves fit for self-government, when they could allow a Stalin to die peacefully in his bed, like any honest man. To this day, some European countries are still so very unripe that for decades now they have not been able to exist without a Franco or a Salazar.

The same de Gaulle whose Minister of Information could say: 'France believes that the first condition of peace today is non-intervention. . . . No country should interfere in the domestic affairs of another country', thought nothing contradictory in sending his troops to interfere in Gabonese internal affairs. The Americans, who so firmly believe that 'all men are created equal', took more than a century to grasp the argument that a slightly bigger nose, woollier hair and just that little more pigment in the skin should not make a person less equal than the 'all men'. The French might pity or contemn the Congolese today for being unable to keep a stable government. But they themselves have had their bloody revolutions, and, not so long ago, they were lucky if any of their governments saw two full moons at a stretch.

But, having made these points, I ask: Why did we spend so much time learning history in school, if the bitter experiences of others cannot open our eyes to the mistakes we should avoid?

SIX

Revolutionary Situations: II

All newly independent states are understandably proud and jealous of their national sovereignty. Many Africans therefore were gratified when Chou En-lai said, in the last of his 'Principles' for Africa: 'China holds that the sovereignty of African countries should be respected by all other countries, and that encroachment and interference from any quarter should be opposed.' As it stands, this principle can be interpreted both as a warning to all outsiders who might seek to encroach on our sovereignty, and as an exhortation to us to oppose with the utmost vigour any meddling from outside.

As it stands, it is excellent. But, as I have already pointed out, we must not take at its face value Peking's claim that 'in its relations with African countries, China has consistently and unswervingly taken [her] stand in accordance with the Five Principles of Peaceful Coexistence'. In judging China by my concept of what constitutes an infringement of sovereignty, I would normally tend to apply Western standards, my education having been mainly Western in pattern. To offset this acquired

bias of my mind, I have elected to measure Chinese actions by
a communist yardstick.

In an open letter, published in *Pravda* on July 14, 1963, the
Central Committee of the Communist Party of the Soviet Union
said that 'contrary to the standards of friendly relations between
fraternal Socialist countries, [the Chinese comrades] have begun with increasing importunity and persistence to spread
illegally in Moscow and other Soviet cities' literature attacking the policy and motives of the Soviet government. The
Russian communists called attention to 'the impermissibility
of such actions, which crudely violate the sovereignty of our
state'.

Also, on February 6, 1966, Fidel Castro directly accused the
Red Chinese of having committed many unsocialist sins
including the violation of his country's sovereignty through
the distribution in Cuba of unauthorised propaganda material.

So there we are. I contend that, if distributing anti-Soviet
literature in the Soviet Union and Cuba constitutes a violation
of sovereignty, then the training, advising and equipping of
local guerrilla fighters to overthrow an African government
must be far more serious infringements of sovereignty.

Some readers may think this a rather academic way of
approaching the problem of revolutionary situations within
African states. It is far from being so. For us, the problem is not
simply the local situation in itself, but the opportunities our
internal difficulties and dissensions give to outsiders who wish
to use the situation for their own ends. And these outsiders are
never more dangerous than when they talk about their respect
for our sovereignty.

I shall now survey a few of the revolutionary situations that
have actually led to mutual strife. The countries included in this
survey are not necessarily those whose revolutionary situations
are of the most acute type; but, taken together, they all repre-
sent different aspects of the general phenomenon of internal
unrest in Africa in relation to subversive activities from outside.

In this context, let us explore in further detail the activities of the Red Chinese in Africa.

CONGO

Undoubtedly the Chinese leaders have found more revolutionary situations of their 'chaos and confusion' type among the newly independent areas of our continent than in the still-colonial portions. The Congo provides the classic—and tragic—example. It was with troubled hearts that, in 1960, African peoples saw the Congo slide into chaos and civil war. The enemies of African freedom hailed this as a demonstration of how unfitted we were for self-rule, conveniently ignoring the criminal failure of the Belgians to give their colonial subjects higher educational and administrative experience. African governments separately and in concert did what they could to bring order to the Congo (though some among them were busier undoing than doing). United Nations troops came in, but the situation continued confused for some considerable time. It was just when the United Nations felt able to conclude its peace-keeping operations in the Congo that Peking catapulted Mulele on to the scene.

Pierre Mulele, principal actor in the Kwilu revolt, was born in 1929 at Kulu-Matendu in Oriental Province, of the Bambunda tribe. He left the mission school in Kinzambi rather than recant some allegedly heretical religious ideas he had been preaching to his fellow students. He afterwards joined the army, but had to leave it to avoid being arrested by the Belgians, who had discovered that he was studying how to organise mutinies. After much difficulty, Mulele got to Leopoldville, where he found a job as a government clerk. In the capital he became friendly with Varius, the Czechoslovak consul, who gave him the rudiments of Marxist doctrine. On a trip to Guinea in 1959, he made the acquaintance of Mme Blouin, a prominent figure in African Marxist circles.

A conflict afterwards broke out between Mulele and the

leadership of the Parti Solidaire Africain in Kwilu Province when he endeavoured to make them adopt this Marxist doctrine. When Congo became independent, Lumumba made Mulele Minister of Education, but while his Prime Minister was away at the United Nations, Mulele urged Gizenga, the Vice-Premier, to seize power because he considered that Lumumba paid too much attention to Belgian and Western opinion. The plot failed, but shortly afterwards the Lumumba government collapsed. Mulele hurried to Kivu Province, where he helped Gizenga to form the Stanleyville government, which claimed to be the *de jure* government of the Congo.* He became this government's representative in Cairo.

In March 1962, Mulele left Cairo for a visit to Prague, the purpose of which was to ask the Czechoslovak government for aid in organising sabotage, assassination and terrorist activities in the Congo. He also requested training for himself in the use of explosives. The Czechs, however, could not see their way to sending an instructor to him in Cairo. In May 1962, the Chinese ambassador in Egypt, Chen Chia-kang, announced that Mulele and another Congolese, Theodore Bengila, were in Peking. The two of them started a course in guerrilla warfare and Marxist ideology.

* I was in Peking when the representative of Gizenga's Stanleyville government arrived there. We African students weren't sure, and didn't care to find out, what his status was in exact diplomatic terms. We simply called him the Congolese ambassador, and he didn't correct us when we addressed him as such. He and his three aides participated fully in the Africa Week celebrations of our Students' Union, the highlight of which was a mass rally protesting against Lumumba's murder and against the imperialists and colonialists. I was told by the Cameroon students, though I neither verified this nor attached much importance to it at the time, that the Gizenga embassy and all its officials were maintained entirely at the expense of the Chinese government. By accepted international diplomatic standards, this would be improper conduct on China's part and would constitute an infringement of Congo sovereignty. At that time, however, Peking recognised Gizenga's government as the only legal government of the Congo.

Most Africans governments send their military personnel to foreign countries for further training. The Nigerians send theirs to Britain, the Ghanaians to Britain (and formerly to Cuba as well), the Somalis to the Soviet Union. These military training schemes are sponsored by the duly constituted government of the country. By the time Mulele and Bengila went to Peking, however, Gizenga's government had disintegrated and, thanks to United Nations action, the situation in the Congo had cleared sufficiently for everybody, even radical African governments, to recognise that the Congo had only one legal government in the field: the central government of Cyrille Adoula. Everybody, that is, except China. Training rebels to oppose the recognised government and reintroduce confusion was the way China sought to deal with the Congo's problems.

The first inkling the Congolese government had of pending trouble came when the gendarmerie discovered a Muleleist training camp at Lukamba in Kwilu Province in September 1963. Mulele started operations in his own tribal area, where he could exploit the feelings of his own people. Congolese politics are tribally dominated to a greater extent than in other parts of Africa, and it is not surprising that the next tribes to fall under his influence after the Bambunda were the Bapenda, Gizenga's tribe, and the Batetela, Lumumba's tribe. Mulele succeeded in convincing these tribes that his revolution aimed at forming a regime headed by Gizenga, and that refusal to support it was tantamount to opposing Gizenga.

Systematically, these tribes murdered all people, village chiefs along with the rest, who opposed Mulele's revolution. Mulele gave orders for the destruction of all institutions: schools, Christian missions, government offices and industrial centres— all establishments, in short, which could imaginably exert any form of political and social influence. For the same reason, school teachers, missionaries, hospital staff, central and provincial government personnel, and even their relatives, became victims of persecution, and, in many cases, were murdered.

The lack of qualified personnel to man all sectors of the administration has been—and still remains—a major weakness of the Congo. Moreover, Belgian educational policy in that country had been such that African education was shouldered almost entirely by foreign missionaries. Without them, not even Lumumba or the leaders of the revolt would themselves have had any education worth mentioning. If Mulele and his men were really seeking a better Congo, the indiscriminate killing of educated Congolese and missionaries was the worst possible way to begin.

A curious, but not altogether surprising aspect of insurgent activity was their use of the *dawa*, a special 'medicine' that was supposed to make the rebel warriors (simbas) bullet-proof. The Batetela and related tribes of Maniema Province have, for a long time, held undisputed first place as the medicine men of this region. As a result, they were much feared by neighbouring tribes, whom they terrorised in collaboration with the Arab slavers of the old days. It is not certain whether the Moscow faction or the Peking faction of the Conseil National de Libération was directly responsible for this revival of superstition and sorcery by the insurgents. But it is well known that courses in this subject are given in the subversion schools of both these communist countries. Since each is as guilty as the other, I shall quote evidence from Moscow, which is more lucid than that from Peking.

Suzanne Labin quotes[1] an interesting story (first published in the London *Sunday Telegraph*) told by a Nigerian named Anthony Okotcha. After completing a course in Marxism-Leninism, he moved on to study 'occult sciences', a section of which, he tells us, was devoted to 'witch doctors'. The first time Okotcha and his wife entered the classroom for their 'witch doctor' course, they found their teacher in the midst of a bizarre collection of plastic human skulls and skeletons. The teacher's introduction to the lesson was: 'You know that in certain underdeveloped countries of Africa, the people are highly superstitious, and one can gain political objectives only by playing on these superstitions.' After pointing out the need to spread those same methods which helped to kindle the Mau Mau revolt in Kenya, and stressing that one single witch doctor operating among primitive peoples can achieve more than a dozen lecturers, the teacher continued: 'You see how far we can get if he is a communist.' The teacher explained how superstitious tribal men could be swayed by making a skeleton speak through a microphone hidden inside it. A sample of what the skeleton could say was: 'I am your ancestral spirit. I command you to go and kill the British governor tonight and bring me his head. If you fail, your family will always live under the evil eye.'

This Nigerian student completed his theoretical course in subversion but refused to commit murder and the other crimes that the Nigerian Communist Party had ordered. It is common knowledge, however, that the Congolese insurgents used these revived superstitions with great effect, causing Congolese army regulars to flee in mortal terror.

The *Peking Review*, in an article captioned "Rising Armed Struggle in the Congo", admiringly described how the 'Congolese liberators . . . follow eight simple and straightforward rules' in their military operations. The eight rules are: 1. Respect for people; 2. Honest purchase from villagers; 3. Due return of everything borrowed; 4. Payment for anything damaged; 5. Refraining from maltreating or abusing others; 6. Refraining from destroying or damaging villagers' farmland; 7. Respect for women and refraining from insulting them; 8. Refraining from maltreatment of prisoners of war, and from confiscating their personal belongings, such as rings, money, watches and other personal possessions.[2]

Now, these eight rules of the 'Congolese liberators'—observed with the fidelity we have noted!—are the same, point for point, as those of China's Red Army, except for minor changes in the text to suit local conditions. Mulele could, of course, have read

Mao and devised his own version of the Chinese leader's guerrilla warfare precepts. But his lecture notes on guerrilla tactics, captured by the Congolese army, indicate clearly the direct involvement of Peking in his campaign.

China gave immediate propaganda support to Mulele when he started his revolt in earnest in January 1964, but from the following month they were able to do more. Vying with the Soviet Union, Peking adopted a section of the Conseil National de Libération, which was directing the revolt. They set up a six-man mission in Brazzaville, across the river from Leopold-ville (Kinshasa), where discredited Congolese politicians, led by Christophe Gbenye and Egide Bocheley Davidson, had set up the CNL. From this mission, the Chinese were able directly to influence the course of the revolt.*

Peking-supported camps for guerrillas were set up at Gambona and Impfondo, where Congolese 'freedom fighters', trained in China since 1961, acted as instructors. Later they were joined by Chinese instructors and members of the embassy in Brazza-ville. Colonel Kan Mai, counsellor at the embassy, is reputed to have been one of the driving forces behind the insurgents. In May 1964, a 75-kilowatt radio transmitter arrived from China and was set up at Pointe Noire in Congo-Brazzaville (the former French Congo). This was part of a plan by Peking to gain control in Brazzaville and also to use it as a base for operations against the Leopoldville government. The radio transmitter beamed propaganda to Leopoldville and to the eastern Congo. In June a leader of the CNL returned from Peking with $20,000 in aid for his organisation.

At the same time, the Chinese were developing their position in Burundi to give them another base for operations in the Congo. Details of their activities in Bujumbura, capital of Burundi, are given later in this chapter. What we need to note here is the Chinese attempt to link the revolutionary situations in this part of

* Chinese intervention in the Congo has been handled through their embassies in Brazzaville, Bujumbura (Burundi) and Dar-es-Salaam.

Africa, using the various states which flank the Congo as spring-boards for their subversive activities in this unfortunate country.

In January 1964, Gaston Soumialot was ordered by Gbenye of the CNL to install a 'Lumumbist' government in Kivu Province. By May there was a full-scale rising in this part of eastern Congo, controlled at the start by Soumialot from Burundi. He operated from the same hotel which then housed members of the Chinese mission. Before Congo's independence in 1960, Soumialot had been manager of a grocery store. He entered politics in 1959 as director of press and propaganda in Lumumba's Mouvement National Congolais. With indepen-dence, he became district commissioner of his home area, but was dismissed on charges of misappropriation of funds, political interference and ordering arbitrary arrests. Four months later he was imprisoned for promoting tribal disputes. He was subsequently released and made Minister of Justice in Antoine Omari's provincial government in Kivu. But he was soon dis-missed again, and little was heard of him until the Kivu revolt broke out in 1964.

As it turned out, the subversive activities of the Chinese and Mulele and Soumialot did not achieve the success Peking desired. The fall of Stanleyville to Congolese government forces in November 1964 led to the flight of the insurgent leaders to the Sudan. The initiative in fomenting revolution passed, for the moment at least, to the Russians, the Algerians and the Egyptians, who organised an airlift of arms and supplies, and a training programme in the Sudan for the insurgents.

Peking did not let itself be discouraged by this setback, nor by the elimination of its base in Bujumbura when the Burundi government, exasperated by Chinese subversion against it, expelled the mission there. Dar-es-Salaam in Tan-zania next became a main centre of Chinese activity. The CNL had already, in July 1964, sent a representative to organise a supply base in Dar-es-Salaam. The Chinese began to show marked interest in the railway from Dar-es-Salaam to Kigoma on the eastern shores of Lake Tanganyika eighty miles above Albertville in the Congo. The Congolese insurgents are thought to have been put in contact with the Zanzibari 'freedom fighters' and the men the Chinese were training on the island of Pemba. Chinese supplies for the CNL insurgents apparently were routed through Dar-es-Salaam.

And there was still Mulele. After the fall of Stanleyville, he had been presumed dead, but before long he showed he was still very much alive. He placed himself, with about 5,000 men, at the disposal of Egide Bocheley Davidson, who claimed to have been elected to the leadership of the CNL in preference to Gbenye. The latter, with Soumialot, sought help from African countries. Mulele's band of guerrillas did not. China was their inspirer and helper.

Although the forces of the central government of the Congo have succeeded in consolidating their control, the insurgents cannot be assumed to be permanently disabled or contained. As late as the spring of 1966, Chinese agents were known to be active in maintaining contact with potential insurgent leaders in an effort to bring about an effective regrouping of the dissident forces under a centralised (and Chinese-controlled) command. Peking apparently still hoped to use Burundi as a base for a Congo come-back, even though it had—temporarily, at least—lost its diplomatic base there.

Not that we should assume automatically that Mulele and his kind have acted consciously as the henchmen of a foreign power. While Peking thought it was using such men for its own ends, they thought they were using Peking for their own ambitions. It would also be a great mistake to ascribe the upheavals in the Congo solely to the machinations of the Chinese or any other external power. Congolese tribes nurse a multitude of feuds that have origin in the pre-colonial past. Add to these intertribal enmities the scarcity of trained personnel —leading to incompetence in central and provincial governments, and which, in its turn, makes the hand of authority almost unfelt

in the wild and remote areas, or felt only in its more odious forms
—and you have the makings of any number of situations
favourable for revolts and disturbances. The unemployed
politicians left over by the Lumumba and Gizenga governments
knew this weakness very well and exploited it to the full.

Lumumba's earlier and very unwise promise that, after
independence, all Congolese would 'turn white'—that is, grow
rich, live in luxurious villas and drive about in fine cars, just
like the Belgians and other white settlers—had not materialised.
It was easy enough for unscrupulous politicians to convince
ignorant tribesmen that these promises would have come true
had not Lumumba been killed by the perfidious men in Leopoldville, and to incite them to take up arms on behalf of those
claiming to be Lumumba's political heirs.

The revolutionary situation was there all the time. But it
needed moral and material support from abroad to initiate and
maintain revolutionary action. China, the Soviet Union and
the so-called progressive African countries took it upon themselves to supply—bountifully—this support and encouragement. Without the interference of outside forces, the Congolese
scene during the post-independence period would have been less
turbulent, and any disturbances would have been put down
at much less cost of lives and property, and without the help
of the hated white mercenaries.

The Congo, that backward giant of Africa, has untold natural
resources. It is only in peace and stability that these can be
tapped for the benefit of the Congolese. Any element that
threatens this peace and stability, as the Chinese have done,
is certainly an element hostile to Africa.

RWANDA AND BURUNDI

For another 'revolutionary situation' that appealed to the
Chinese, consider Rwanda and Burundi: this time not in the
context of springboards towards the Congo but as trouble-spots
in themselves.

More than four centuries ago, legend has it, a band of Tutsi tribesmen migrated up the valley of the Upper Nile, driving before them great herds of long-horned white zebus. On the eastern shores of Lake Tanganyika and Lake Kivu, they came upon the Bahutu, who—so the story goes—were so impressed by the majestic stature of the Watutsi* that they volunteered to herd their no less majestic cattle. Thus did the Bahutu bind themselves into vassalage, and the two countries now known as Burundi and Rwanda (or Urundi and Ruanda as they were called before independence) were ruled by Tutsi kings with the traditional title of Mwami. With the opening up of Central Africa to European colonisation in the late nineteenth century, the two peoples came under Belgian control with the creation of the 'Congo Free State' by the Conference of Berlin of 1885 which sanctioned the partition of Africa.

Though jointly under the control of Belgium, the two countries had separate identities in many ways, and when independence came on July 1, 1962, they became distinct sovereign states. But before independence came, violence had broken out in Rwanda. In that year, reportedly with the con- nivance of the Belgian administrative authorities, the Bahutu, who represented 85 per cent of the population, overthrew the Watutsi ruling minority in a bloody revolt. Mwami Kigeri V fled, first to Uganda—whence he was expelled for subversive activities against a friendly country—and then to Kenya. Also into exile went a number of his courtiers, while thousands of lowlier Watutsi fled to Uganda, Kenya, Burundi, Tanganyika and the Congolese province of Kivu.

At this point, a very interesting person came on to the scene: one Kao Liang. Ostensibly the correspondent for the New China News Agency in Dar-es-Salaam, Kao Liang was in fact the reconnaissance man for the Chinese Ministry of Foreign Affairs. Expelled from India in 1960 for 'unjournalistic activities', his

---

* Watutsi men are about seven feet tall on average. I met a few on my East African tour and can testifiy to their impressive height.

next assignment was in Zanzibar. The *Indian Observer* said of him: 'After his exit from India, he was deputed to Zanzibar, and do you know what happened there?'[3] Of course, an overtly leftist bloody revolution. As a matter of policy, correspondents of the New China News Agency are expected to devote part of their time and talents to such gentle pastimes as spying on and subverting their host countries.

Comrade Kao clearly took the whole of East and Central Africa for his province, and he lost no time in making contact with Tutsi refugees in Burundi and other neighbouring countries. The Tutsi refugees had formed themselves into guerrilla bands called *Inyenzi*—Cockroaches, so known from their raiding by night. The aim was to overthrow the Bahutu Republic of Rwanda and restore to themselves the feudal overlordship they had lost. So confident were they of early success that they stubbornly refused even to cultivate the land offered them by their host governments. Here, Peking's agents found a ready-made and exploitable revolutionary situation.

One would have expected that, having in their doctrine condemned feudalism and subsequently overthrown the feudal overlords in their own country, the Chinese would normally support the Hutus of Rwanda against the reimposition of feudalism. But other considerations were guiding Peking's actions. Communists, Russian and Chinese alike, will opportunistically collaborate with any non-communist movement to achieve their own purposes, after which the non-communist movement is promptly neutralised. It is no surprise, therefore, that the Chinese threw in their lot with the feudalists against the republicans. They were also probably influenced by the fact that the Rwanda Republic is the only African country to have written a specific anti-communist clause into its constitution, and has, moreover, recognised Nationalist China. But the governing factor was the attractive revolutionary situation. Through Kao Liang, Chinese funds and advice reached the *Inyenzi* leaders regularly. Even Mwami Kigeri V himself thought nothing of shedding his pride in order to pick the crumbs that fell from Peking's table. A group of Tutsi guerrillas were taken to Peking for special training. In late 1963, wave after wave of *Inyenzi* invaded Rwanda, seeking to wreak vengeance on their former vassals, now masters of the country. With Belgian help the Rwanda armed forces dealt crushing blows to each of the twelve Tutsi invasion bands, killing an estimated 2,500 Tutsis in a countrywide massacre. Horrible stories were told of the atrocities committed against men, women and children. Crocodiles gorged themselves with Tutsi bodies floating down the Ruzizi river into Lake Tanganyika. At the height of the slaughter, corpses were reported to be floating by at the rate of forty a minute.

Here in Rwanda, as in the former Belgian Congo, the revolutionary situation itself was home-made, but China's exploitation of it makes a total lie of Peking's claim that it respects the sovereignty of African countries.

A key to China's activities, both in respect to Rwanda and to the Congo, was Burundi. Peking needs forward bases for its subversive operations and with easy access for its agents. We have already seen how the Chinese sought to use Congo-Brazzaville for this purpose. It is instructive to see how they proceeded in Burundi.

Diplomatic relations were established between Peking and Bujumbura in December 1963. A Chinese chargé d'affaires and a small staff arrived in January 1964; the ambassador followed in June. The way had been well prepared by Kao Liang, disguised as a journalist, whose distribution of 'gifts' to influential Burundians and highly persuasive tongue had created a strong body of pro-Chinese feeling in official circles. The embassy was first established in the wing of a hotel in Bujumbura but it later moved to a villa surrounded by a high palisade. The embassy staff increased substantially; by October 1964, it was reported to number between eighteen and twenty-two members—far too big for a normal peaceable diplomatic mission from a country, such as China, with so few (ostensible) commitments in Burundi.

The nature of the undercover commitment in Bujumbura was threefold. First, to give aid to the Congolese insurgents. We have seen the effects of the embassy's role in the Congo and Rwanda. China's ambassador in Bujumbura acted as recruiting officer to Soumialot's guerrillas in Kivu, enrolling fighters by giving them a year's pay in advance. A Chinese officer was killed in a clash north of Luluabourg, and two Chinese advisers were reported to be with rebel forces in Uvira. The second purpose was to incite Tutsi refugees against Rwanda, and we now know the horrifying outcome of that effort. But this was not all; the third objective of the Bujumbura mission was to subvert the very country to whose government it was accredited. Respect for 'national sovereignty'? Burundi was soon to learn the true meaning of Chou's high-sounding words.

Peking's subversion was of the classic communist type. Potential tools among Burundian officials and ordinary citizens were sought out, presented with gifts and conditioned by skilful propaganda. Regular payments were made to trade union and youth movement leaders. Peking hospitality was laid on for suitable Burundians who could be impressed. Peking even offered to improve the country's road system: an offer which sounds like a really useful form of help unless you know that the objective is to penetrate every part of the country and make contacts for intelligence and subversion.

Things were going well for Peking—too well, as it developed. On December 19, 1964, the Burundian Prime Minister, Nyamoya, who had shown himself a cordial friend of the Chinese embassy in Bujumbura, was removed by a vote of censure in the parliament, accusing him of despotism, nepotism and interference with justice. Early in January, he was replaced by a new Prime Minister, Pierre Ngendandumwe. Only ten days later Ngendandumwe was assassinated. Although no evidence of Chinese involvement in the political murder came to light, the new government, already perturbed at Chinese activity among its nationals, grew even more alarmed when its arrests of suspected persons uncovered large supplies of ammunition. These, it reckoned, were as likely to be destined for dissident Burundians as for Congolese or Rwandan insurgents.

The Chinese had overplayed their hand. Their involvement in the Congo rebellion had become plain for all to see. No less plain now were their machinations in Burundi itself. The Burundian government broke off diplomatic relations with Peking and expelled the staff of the embassy in Bujumbura. Thus the Chinese lost the key point in their campaign for Central Africa—for the time being, at least. Nevertheless, with so many friends, or gullible innocents, elsewhere in Africa, the continent's 'revolutionary prospects' continued 'excellent' for them.

CAMEROON

Contrary to the wishes of the government of the Cameroon Republic, the Chinese have, for several years, been giving military training in China to dissident Cameroonians. In mid-1961, reports revealed the military training given to six Cameroonians in a ten-week course in 1960. The theory and practice of guerrilla warfare and combat tactics were taught them, and they were also instructed in how to make and use explosives, how to blow up bridges, buildings, railways and vehicles and how to sabotage airfields and telephone communications, power stations and wireless installations. All this, together with tuition in setting ambushes, fortifying villages, infiltrating key positions and dealing with political opponents, constitutes a pretty complete course in subversion.

The Chinese did not spend their time and money on this group of Cameroonians simply for the joy of imparting useful knowledge. The six men brought back with them from China documents containing detailed instructions for putting their lessons into practice. The authorities found out about this and

arrested them. The Cameroonian delegate at the United
Nations protested in December 1961 against China's infringe-
ment of his country's sovereignty, and outlined the extent of
Peking's interference in its internal affairs:

> Guerrilla weapons and many propaganda pamphlets which
> have been seized and are still being seized enable us beyond
> a shadow of doubt, to establish the responsibility of Peking in
> leading and equipping localised underground groups in the
> Cameroon. . . . Many young Cameroonians, inveigled and led
> by China under false pretexts, receive there psychological
> and military preparations for the ultimate goal of being sent
> back to our national territory to engage in subversive
> activities and to serve as the instructors and personnel in an
> eventual general rebellion.

He was referring to extremists in the Union des Populations
du Cameroun (UPC), members of which had been allowed to
return to the country and resume legal political activities. China
saw in the UPC a valuable instrument for her policies, and in
November 1961 Mao Tse-tung himself said that his government
had 'for a long time supported the fight' of the UPC and that
'the Chinese people will continue to assist this movement in its
fight to the bitter end'. Peking's interference in Cameroonian
affairs was so blatant that there could be no question of the
country's delegation supporting the admission of Communist
China to the United Nations. 'China fosters the Cameroonian
rebellion', said President Ahidjo, 'and thus we cannot speak
out in favour of its admission to the UN because it does not fulfil
the fundamental conditions prescribed in the Charter.' His
government affirmed that it would maintain this attitude as
long as that situation existed.

But, so far, Chinese ambitions in the Cameroon have been
frustrated, mainly because, from Peking's point of view, the
UPC has proved a broken reed. The Union, subjected to the rival
pressures and machinations of pro-Russian and pro-Chinese

factions acting as instruments of the two great rivals in the Sino-Soviet conflict, came near to complete disintegration. Its Revolutionary Committee in Accra in September 1964, expressed bitter disillusionment with the Chinese, declaring that they 'had assumed a hostile attitude towards [the UPC], had grossly interfered in the UPC's internal affairs and had supported opportunist elements which opposed its leadership'. All of which meant that, for the time being at least, Peking had lost out to Moscow in the contest for the leadership of 'revolutionary elements' in the Cameroon Republic.

◙   ◙

We have seen how, by professions of friendship and offers of aid, China has sought to use newly independent states in Africa as tools for her ambitions in the continent. Is it to be assumed, then, that every African state which accepts Chinese diplomatic missions and technical assistance is, knowingly or unknowingly, a pawn in Mao's hand? Some of us might be tempted to say 'Yes' to this in view of the kind of experiences I have just recounted. In fact, matters are not quite so simple as that. A new state needs help in so many ways. A wise national leader will not want to have all his eggs in one basket, particularly if he genuinely seeks to maintain a position of non-alignment in the international ideological cold war. The test of his wisdom is the degree to which he can use the gift-bearing foreign power without being used by it. His ability to avoid being made a tool of will largely depend on his strength as a just ruler of a just and united society. So far, China's subversive policies have come near to success in states suffering from post-independence weaknesses and internal tensions; in short, states where the 'revolutionary situation' actually or latently exists. It would be a woefully defeatist pessimism to assume that *no* African state is capable, without becoming a subverted pawn, of having diplomatic and aid-providing relations with the great and 'perilous' powers—Western, Russian or Chinese.

For example, the presence of eleven Chinese army instructors in Tanzania has been viewed with alarm by many Western observers. This is a good example of the situation where cool appraisal, not rash assumption, is needed. It has been argued that this military aid constitutes a breach of Tanzania's sovereignty. If such aid were secret or exclusive of similar aid from other countries, then one's alarmed suspicions would be justified. But, as President Nyerere has pointed out, if there is a group of Chinese giving military training to Tanzanian forces, there are also similar groups from Canada, Britain and Germany. That some Western observers should leap to the assumption that Nyerere is a 'pawn' of the Chinese only shows that, when convenient to them, they are prone to adopt the same double standard of which they accuse Africans.

Here is an illustration. In November 1964, Belgian paratroops, flown in American planes, went to war-torn Stanleyville and Paulis to rescue men, women and children of diverse nationalities. You may call this a 'humanitarian mission' or an 'imperialist intervention', according to the side you are on. I do not intend to reopen the argument about the moral justification for this operation. I only want to refer to the justification used by the Western powers, which is that, because the central Congolese government had given its consent for the operation, it did not therefore constitute either an intervention or an infringement of sovereignty. If this argument justifies the Western powers' brief but far-reaching presence in the Congo, it can also justify the Chinese presence in Tanzania, where it exists by the specific decision of the country's government. To condemn an African leader because he receives Chinese economic aid or chooses to invite Chinese technicians is the kind of patronising attitude that once led the former colonial masters to forbid us to read or learn anything from other countries but their own. There is every evidence that Africans have been learning a great deal from their ideological flirtations, and that, left to ourselves, we can discover soon enough who our real friends are.

However, there has been at least one instance when, even though present by the express invitation of a government, the Chinese stepped sharply on someone's sovereign toes. This was the case in Ghana, where Nkrumah invited the Chinese to train men in his secret guerrilla camps.

NKRUMAH'S GHANA

It all began on August 5, 1964, with an agreement reached between Nkrumah's government and that of Red China. Signed for China by Huang Hua and for Ghana by E. O. Baah, the single-page agreement provided in its Article 1 for the sending of a Chinese military mission to Ghana; in Article 2 for the duration of its stay, which was to be two years unless extended; and in Article 3 for the maintenance costs of the mission to be paid by the Ghanaian government.

All this was certainly no infringement of Ghanaian sovereignty, save in the technical sense that, at the material moment, Nkrumah had morally ceased to be the true representative of his people. However, as this whole operation—appropriately named 'Operation Green Mamba' after that deadliest of snakes—began to unfold, it became apparent that at stake was the sovereignty of every independent African country.[4] Chinese diplomatic missions all over Africa obligingly dispatched to Accra young Africans reliable in their ideological sympathies towards China.

It would have been understandable if training facilities had been extended solely to nationals of Africa's still-dependent territories. Nkrumah might then have been hailed as a great and selfless African nationalist, for all that Ghanaians had a very low opinion of the man who had brought his country to the verge of starvation and economic ruin while insisting on breasting a problem that properly belonged to the Organisation of African Unity. But, as it was, men from Cameroon, Rwanda, Tanzania, Zambia, Nigeria, Niger, Togo, Guinea, the two Congos, Ivory Coast and many other African independent states flocked into Nkrumah's guerrilla training camps and his Ideological Institute. This left no room to doubt that his aim was conquest by brute force where he had failed by persuasion.

Arms and ammunition destined for the guerrilla trainees began to arrive in Ghana under the false label of 'medical supplies' donated by the Chinese people. The unwitting Ghanaian people received these 'gifts' with as much fanfare as the Indonesians welcoming supplies of 'building materials' from China that turned out to be arms in large quantities. In Indonesia, these kind 'gifts' from China quietly went into the hands of the Indonesian communists, who were thus equipped to start the coup of September 30, 1965—which backfired to their utter discomfiture. In Ghana, the arms were stockpiled against the day when 'Operation Green Mamba' would find its final culmination in the military invasion of other African countries, whose only wish was to be left in peace to grapple with their crushing economic problems.

Emboldened by the success achieved within the first year of operation, the Sino-Nkrumah conspiracy hatched other audacious plans. One of these called for a number of saboteurs, disguised as civilian passengers, to travel by direct flight to another African country and, on landing, to seize and hold the airport long enough for reinforcements to arrive by air. And that would have been another country fallen into the clutches of the Chinese with the aid of their Little Brother in Accra.

But, as the world now knows, these warlike preparations and the domestic difficulties brought on the Ghanaian people by Nkrumah's foolishness became too much for Ghana's armed forces and police to stomach. They struck, and Ghana was saved. Many of her neighbours were thus spared the horrors of foreign-incited bloody revolution.

If any kind of foreign aid calls loudly and clearly for condemnation, this is it.

◙   ◙

Thus we see how Red China treats with utter contempt the sovereignty of African countries by acting in collusion with those national leaders whom ambition or gullibility makes blind to the interests of their own people and their fellow Africans.

To Chou En-lai, Africans must have appeared to be half-wits, prepared to accept all his words at face-value. Why else would he tour our countries distributing pleasant smiles he never wears at home, and making us a gift of the same 'Five Principles' that China used to lure India and other countries into a false sense of security before striking them in the back?

Africa is at present a continent of baffled peoples: baffled by the enormity of the tasks and problems that confront them in national development. We need to be left in peace to think out our problems and regain our composure. This is not a favour we have to beg from any foreign power. It is a right: our right to be left alone if we so wish.

But we also need help, and that urgently; which means that we need friends, sincere friends.

What kind of friend is that foreign power that holds us at gunpoint?

SEVEN

Invitation to Backwardness

All the independent countries of our African continent have one 'revolutionary situation' in common: a desperate need for economic development and an awareness of our incapacity for achieving such development through our own single-handed efforts—regardless of who our current leaders may be.

I see great merit in Chou En-lai's statement that 'in national reconstruction reliance must mainly be placed on the strength of one's own country, and foreign aid is only auxiliary'. But the merit remains for only so long as the statement is considered in isolation. When seen in relation to what is actually taking place in world affairs, the 'catch' becomes obvious. This could possibly explain why, during his speech in Mogadishu on February 3, 1964, Chou tried to pass off the same statement by preluding it with 'many African friends have pointed out that in national reconstruction. . . .' I am going to devote some attention to this important statement on foreign aid and self-reliance.

In dealing with foreign aid to Africa, it is necessary to bear two points in mind. The first is that, in ninety-nine cases out of

a hundred, there is no such thing as disinterested aid or aid
without strings. The second is that foreign aid to African
countries is inextricably mixed up with two levels of ideological
and power struggle: the East-West tug-of-war and that very
confusing Sino-Soviet shindig.

AID WITH STRINGS

Strings attached to foreign aid may be of two kinds: strings
implicit and strings explicit. It may clarify the matter to
consider, first of all, what happens in personal life when one
individual seeks help from another. If a friend in dire need
asks me for a loan, I may gain several things by granting it.
My self-esteem may be increased and I may establish or enhance
my reputation for open-handedness. If he is a very close friend,
I shall have the pleasure of helping someone I like. But I shall
also expect, if I in turn should stand in need, financial or otherwise, that he will help me. I shall expect, furthermore, that he
will demonstrate his gratitude to me in some way. Thus, I lay
a moral obligation on anybody to whom I do a favour. I place
him in a position where it is assumed that he will return the
kindness at a favourable opportunity. This presupposes, of
course, that the recipient is genuinely grateful and acknowledges
moral obligations. Perhaps also I am business-minded and put
a small interest on the loan.

All these things are 'strings', even when they remain un-
spoken wishes and hopes. If, for some reason or other, I come
to regard my friend as an ingrate, he will find it difficult to get
a loan another time. These attitudes to our neighbours run
through the actions of most men. Even 'selfish' people may be
induced to give a helping hand by the prospect of future
benefits, or by expectations of a reward in the next world.

The motives and reactions of governments in international
affairs are, of course, much more complex than my simple
personal example, but since governments and societies are
made up of men, the same general trends run through inter-

national relations. I would therefore define strings on aid as any obligation—financial or political, positive or negative, moral or otherwise—which emanates from the recipient, voluntarily or involuntarily, and is in the interest of the donor. A few examples will suffice to illustrate this.

France withdrew all her aid to Guinea (not forgetting to pull out the telephone fixtures) when that country voted 'Non' in the 1958 referendum. France also ceased to give aid to Tunisia in 1964 because the latter had nationalised all foreign-owned land, including land owned by French nationals. Besides expecting her former colonies to 'behave', she also expects them to pay back aid by diplomatic favours, such as voting with France in the United Nations and supporting her international policies.

In this category also is the relation between the United States and Cuba. The Americans hope to make the Cubans understand that, where butter for the Cuban bread is concerned, it is much better that it be buttered in the West, and best of all by the United States. To press this point home, America withholds all aid from Cuba, and tries to ensure that her allies do likewise. This policy, however, has had the adverse effect of driving the Cubans further from the United States rather than bringing them back, chastened.

The Soviet Union withdrew the roubles from China, hoping to prove to Peking the impossibility of having two socialist camps as 'self-reliant' entities. All the Russians achieved was to make the Chinese hammer in more firmly the tent-pegs of their newly formed camp. As negative in its results was the American refusal to aid Guinea in 1958, for fear of displeasing France. This sent the Guineans looking 'elsewhere'. (I must confess it is not so easy to put a finger on similar instances in British aid policy. If you are reluctant to declare them innocent of neo-colonialism of this kind, it must be assumed that, as usual, they are too clever to get caught.)

The major aim of the Western powers in granting us aid is to prevent any dangerous (in their view) rapprochments with the Eastern bloc. They know us well enough not to nurse any illusion about our adopting wholesale their point of view. They know we don't owe it to them to stay in *their* camp, and I believe they will be perfectly satisfied if we do not go too far the other way politically. In the economic field, they are interested in keeping the markets they already have in their former colonies and in ensuring that they continue to have the whole or a sizeable share of our agricultural and mineral products.

The Eastern powers, on the other hand, apart from trying to make us move further from the West, to which we were all close at the time of independence, would positively desire to see us adopt their system, and they strive to achieve that end even by means which are not directly connected with aid. Their efforts fall within the framework of the policy of international communism. Besides these political considerations, the countries of the Eastern bloc are very interested in establishing and developing trade relations with African countries. Since most of our pre-independence trade contacts were with the West, they of the East have difficulty sometimes in inducing us to change traditional trade patterns. On the other hand, they have the advantage of coming fresh to the field, without any previous record of sharp-dealing or exploitation to sour our minds towards them.

It will be worth while to wade (just to the ankles) into the Sino-Soviet dispute to examine an interesting aspect of it. China has often accused the Soviet Union of strengthening the position of 'bourgeois' governments through foreign aid programmes. (You may, at this point, want to know what the Chinese mean by 'bourgeois'. If you do not accept Marxist-Leninist doctrine as your principal political tenet, or if you accept this but do not agree with the Chinese Communist Party's interpretation of it in all respects, or if your shirt is too new and too clean and your shoes too shiny—then you are 'bourgeois'. By that definition, all African countries fall into this class.) Because communist propaganda thrives best in places where there is widespread poverty and ignorance, anything which helps to raise the people out of the mire diminishes in the same measure the chances of success of such propaganda. In other words, the more rapidly we advance, economically and educationally, the less sense we will see in revolutionary theories such as those preached by China, and the more difficult it will be for any foreign power to establish its hegemony over us.

The Soviet Union, therefore, in so far as its involvement in Africa is helping our countries to find their own economic feet, is working directly counter to the principles and policies of the world communist movement and is causing a big headache to China, aspirant leader of 'we coloured peoples'. It is not very difficult, though, to understand why the Russians push on with the aid. People are usually more kindly disposed to their benefactors than to others who have done them no favours. The gain accruing from the rapprochement between donor and recipient is expected to more than offset the harm done to the communist movement. Of greater interest still is the fact that China herself gives aid to 'bourgeois' countries, even though she vociferously condemns such aid when given by others.

'Free gifts' such as our needy countries sometimes receive are, at first glance, very attractive. But look a little closer. It is not very difficult to say 'damn you' to a person who makes you a loan. After all, he is going to get his money back, usually with some interest too. The actual 'gift' you receive from the loan-donor is the convenience to you, not the money or the material you take from him. Without his money or materials, which you are going to pay back, you could not carry out your plans at the time most convenient to you. Unaided, Nigeria would have had to wait a few decades to assemble the money and engineers needed to build the Kainji Dam; but aided, she is doing it *now*. This is what all African countries are after: hire-purchase development. We enjoy the benefits now and pay later. A 'free gift', on the other hand, has far greater potentialities of being used for exerting pressure, because the recipient cannot so easily regard himself, as in the case of a loan, as an equal who is in only temporary difficulty. In other words, what the recipient exchanges for the 'free gift' is his pride and his full liberty of action towards the donor. He sells his right to say 'damn you'.

It is clear, therefore, that foreign aid from any quarter whatever may, if the donors are so disposed, be used for exerting political and moral pressure, active or passive.

But the question arises as to how far we are justified in our expectation of receiving without giving anything back. In the case of the former colonialists—Britain, France, Belgium and the rest—it makes some sense to argue that they are repaying a debt. They extracted much wealth from our countries and obtained a host of concessions from us at a time when we were not in a position to exact adequate compensation. Now is the time for them to unburden their consciences by making some requital in terms of pounds and francs. The biblical exhortation to give liberally to the poor might be reason enough to make us expect aid from Western powers that never colonised us. But this cannot apply to the non-believers in the East who never owned colonies in Africa. On the whole, it seems to me both illogical and immoral to apply for aid while stating, or implying, at the same time that we positively will not give anything back. This is not the first illogical thing in African affairs, however!

Again, there is the question of whether it is wise to continue to receive foreign aid when we are fully aware of the dangers it entails. Of course, if we were to think too intently about strings that are or might be attached to foreign aid, we would probably be driven to refusing almost all aid. But such extreme concern is not necessary. Some of the effects of foreign aid strings are so long-term that they may be counter-acted before they do any real harm. Others can be absorbed without appreciable ill effects. And some of those strings are actually in our favour, being conditions required by the donor in order to ensure that, as far as possible, the money given is specifically used on the development projects envisaged. I think quite kindly of such strings when I remember some of the things our politicians have been doing for themselves with money intended for *our* benefit.

There will, however, come a time when our debts will be so heavy that most of the aid we receive will go into repaying previous loans and the interest on them. India is reported to be faced with such a problem already. Of the foreign aid India receives today, fully 60 per cent goes into repaying loans and loan-interest. Closer home, Ghana is experiencing similar difficulties. For a developing country this is a calamity indeed. The one way to avoid such a situation is to deploy foreign aid on projects like agricultural development, irrigation, hydro-electric schemes and industrial enterprises—projects of a kind that can, in the long term, help pay off the loans.

It is very distressing to see the way some African governments fritter away in prestige items the little money they are able to borrow. Some of our ambassadors ride in much more luxurious automobiles than the ambassadors of the countries that grant us aid; their banquets are more sumptuous, their residences more palatial. Our ministers and politicians pay themselves more princely salaries than either our state coffers allow or our countries' living standards warrant. And what do we want with imposing stadia and permanently half-empty hotels that cannot pay their way? What is desirable is aid that helps to make us less dependent; aid that accomplishes anything less than this is undesirable.

Moreover, because of the 10 per cent *solatium* that many of our ministers receive from contractors, the greater the capital cost of a project, the better they like it. Its viability and its relation to the people's life become questions of minor interest. And we are familiar with the case of African rulers who spend the greater part of foreign loans on monuments to their important selves, only to discover, belatedly, that further loans are not easy to obtain and past ones difficult to repay.

It might be interesting to compare ourselves with other underdeveloped countries that also receive foreign aid. Let us take the example of Cuba. Soviet aid to Cuba alone totalled $1,870 million over a three-year period. Military aid accounted for $800 million, economic aid for $470 million, currency support and sugar subsidies for $300 million each.[1] According to a 1963 estimate, Cuba has been receiving Soviet aid at the rate of a million dollars a day. But if we are to judge from the rather disgruntled language some Russians have used to express their feelings ('Cuba alone is sucking us dry'; 'Cuba is a rathole'), socialist Cuba isn't showing much for all the millions she swallows. It is in our interest to ensure that *our* countries do not become ratholes into which foreign helpers pour their gold without a respectable number of dams, schools and highways emerging to bear witness.

Jomo Kenyatta of Kenya certainly knew what he was talking about when he said that, unless capital were invested in his country from abroad, there could be very little development, and that without development there could be no solution to unemployment and no raising of living standards.[2] An article in the West African magazine, *Drum*, wisely observed: 'The success or failure of Nigeria's economic development depends increasingly on the extent of foreign aid. Unless this aid comes through, the development plan will fail. And if the development plan fails, this means goodbye to the hope of raising the standard of living of the Nigerian people.'[3] It quoted very convincing evidence. Of the £700 million and more envisaged for the current six-year development plan, £327 million is expected to come from abroad. You need not read far in any African paper to find expressions of faith in the money of the 'neo-colonialist'. And you will certainly discover, too, that the very countries that are loudest in their condemnation of the neo-colonialists are the ones that are also loudest in their lamentations when the foreign investor, alarmed by their aggressive attitude, turns to seek a more favourable field for his investment.

All over the continent, African governments are working on, or are about to start, enormous economic transformations which would have seemed a flat impossibility a decade ago. These are being achieved with dollars, pounds, francs and roubles from both East and West—often, we must admit, *because* of East-West competition. What this means is that our justifiable concern over the political implications of aid has to be weighed very carefully with the vital necessity of aid for the development of the infrastructure of our economies.

The problem is highlighted by the experience of former French colonies in Africa. Many of the new states in francophone Africa have been accused of aiding neo-colonialism. Let us look briefly at two typical cases.

Dakar, capital of Senegal, was for a long time the administrative centre of the French West African Federation. When the component parts of the Federation became separate states at independence, Senegal found herself saddled with a burdensome administrative structure she did not need and could not afford to maintain. The process of readjusting it to suit Senegal's own needs is still not completed, and the administration continues to eat up the Senegalese revenue, with the result that this single-crop economy (groundnuts) is unable to finance any capital development from its own resources. Congo-Brazzaville is in a very similar dilemma. Its capital city once was the administrative centre for the whole of French Equatorial Africa. With hardly any local industry, and with agricultural and mineral resources largely untapped, the national budget has yet to carry the burden of a large administrative expenditure and of the maintenance of a flamboyant capital city designed for French colonial needs. Hence, there is virtually no go-ahead for Congo-Brazzaville without massive foreign aid.

De Gaulle's France regards giving something for nothing as bad business. Since the francophone states of Africa find it very difficult to get from 'elsewhere' the full equivalent of French aid when they throw out France (Guinea's experience comes to mind), they are forced to accept many of de Gaulle's foreign aid strings. Their compounding the sin of neo-colonialism does not, to my mind, consist in choosing the lesser of two evils— survival at France's apron-strings or total economic collapse— but in not making a consistent and conscientious effort to lessen the degree of their economic dependence. Algeria is perhaps the most notable example of a newly independent state whose ties with the economy of the former colonial power are even tighter than before. France is not only given a virtually free hand in exploiting the mineral resources of the Algerian Sahara; she is even allowed to conduct her nuclear tests there. We thus had the grimly comic spectacle of Ben Bella, self-styled leader of the African revolution, excluding French testing from his con- demnation of the nuclear build-up of the great powers.

Even so, it is all too easy for us in the richer former British territories to pose as saints and point an accusing finger at our much poorer neighbours in the former French colonies. Frankly, I think it is wiser to nibble at the feeder's hand until the whole hand is gone before he wakes up to your game (providing the process doesn't take too long) than to take one chunk of a bite and be cast away in indignation. For the odds are that you may discover that the 'elsewhere' is just as bad or worse, and you may have to grovel back to the old provider.

Foreign aid is by no means confined to intergovernmental schemes; private foreign investors play a very important part also, and the usefulness of their investment is manifold. The taxes they pay to our governments help our development projects; their finished products, when sold locally, save us foreign exchange, and earn us money when sold abroad. Besides helping to relieve the unemployment problem (which can have grave implications when some countries are looking around for revolutionary situations), foreign enterprises help raise the living standards of our people through the wages they pay to their workers. Some foreign enterprises also spend vast sums in on-the-job training schemes which go a long way towards alleviating our shortage of skilled labour and ensure that, eventually, our own people will be able to take over jobs now done by foreign technicians. (In 1963, Britain spent £12·3 million on such training schemes, from which 11,600 Africans benefited.) Moreover, many of these foreign enterprises go into partnership with national development bodies and local businessmen, who thus acquire new business opportunities and techniques.

Of course, foreign enterprises come among us for their own profit, and some of them do not deserve the fertile field that Africa abundantly provides for economic investment. But, now that we have independent governments, we are getting quite a fair share of these profits, together with other things—technical training and business experience—which are, in the long run, more valuable than money.

Whatever else their faults, foreign powers of all species are doing an invaluable, though not necessarily altruistic, job in our countries. The positive neutralism and non-alignment policy of African states, albeit not working exactly as could be desired, tends to make the opposing pulls from East and West counter-balance each other. Foreign aid certainly has its risks, as I have pointed out. But, for us, who have no colonies to plunder, as the European colonialists conveniently had, and who will not consent to become mindless beasts of burden, as has been the case in some non-African countries, foreign aid remains something which we cannot do without at this stage of our history. Besides, the ground it took the present developed countries centuries to cover, we must cover in a few hectic decades or else remain permanently underdeveloped. That is why we cannot depend entirely upon our own resources in the way they could afford to do.

China's Advice

Premier Chou's advice to Africa, quoted at the beginning of this chapter, was given in the cold war context. It is an exhortation to us to refuse aid both from the West and from the Soviet Union. It is pertinent to note that the Chinese did not follow this precious principle of self-reliance when they were at our lowly stage.

Under the Sino-Soviet agreement of friendship, unity and mutual aid signed in Moscow on February 14, 1950, China received long-term credit to the tune of 270 million (new) roubles. The interest was 1 per cent per annum, the most advantageous terms ever offered up to that time by one country to another. Under another agreement covering the period 1950–59, China received a further loan of 117 million roubles, together with aid for the construction or reconstruction of 268 industrial enterprises equipped with the most modern Soviet machinery.

Of the 5,350,000 tons of steel produced in China in 1957, 2,800,000 tons (more than half) came from enterprises built with Soviet aid. China's nuclear device may well prove to have been the result of experience gained in the use of a 10,000 kilowatt atomic reactor and a 24,000,000 electron-volts cyclotron, both built with Russian aid.[4]

In fact, China's entire industrialisation programme for the First Five-Year Plan was geared to and dependent on Soviet aid. Li Fu-chun, chairman of the State Planning Commission, said in mid-1955: 'Of the 156 industrial projects which the Soviet Union is helping us to build, she assists us through the whole process from start to finish.'[5] That the Chinese still consider foreign aid necessary, even at this present time, may be judged from Peking's shrill accusations after the withdrawal of Soviet aid consequent on the breach between Peking and Moscow. China's new baby, 'self-reliance', was not born until the Russians decided that they weren't prepared to dole out any more aid to a country too stubborn to admit the Soviet Union to be the supreme leader of the socialist camp. Looking at it from this angle, China's advice is very reminiscent of the arguments of the fox who, having lost his tail in a trap, tried to convince other foxes that tail-lessness is a decided advantage.

China realises, as do other powers, that Africa is not a model listener to any foreign country that does not bring with it the gold for big dams, steel mills and oil refineries. The West and the Soviet Union have the money and technicians we need, while China is at a big disadvantage in matters of aid because of her comparative poverty and backwardness. Hence her preference for offering us revolutions when what we need is money. The Soviet Union, in its argument with China, tends to take the line that, as well as encouraging 'national liberation' movements, the communist camp must show that it has made great successes in economic construction, thereby strengthening communism's appeal to Africans. Certainly, the Soviet Union's experience of 'from clogs to spacecraft' in forty years does look very attractive to the underdeveloped countries and, undoubtedly, the Russian argument is much more sophisticated and shrewd than the Chinese.

Yet we should look very carefully at the actual experience of communist states when they commend as a necessary example to us their achievements in both 'self-reliance' and economic construction. It can be argued that, after half a century of communist farming, Russia's urgent need for imported Canadian wheat detracts somewhat from the glamour of moon-landings; for every Russian in orbit there are multitudes of his fellow-countrymen with sharp, recent experience of tightened belts.

The advantages of co-operative farming methods are urged on us, but it pays to enquire exactly what is meant by co-operative farming. Certainly, there is evidence in plenty of the excellent good sense of farmers' pooling their resources and joining together in production and marketing co-operatives, and there is much we in Africa can learn from countries, like Denmark, which have such schemes. But in communist countries—in Russia no less than in China—the advantages of co-operative farming have all too often been vitiated by rigid dogmatism about principles and methods, by bad planning and stark inefficiency. The state farms on the communist model have often been too large, the administration excessively complex, and the book-keeping chaotic. The 'virgin lands' scheme in the Soviet Union has created dust-bowls and China's agricultural production falls far short of the needs of the rapidly increasing population.

In both cases, the removal of the land from the ownership of the peasants has deprived them of the incentive to farm intensively and thriftily. In the end, both Russia and China have had to indulge in a bit of revisionism and bring back an element of private farming and the profit motive to get agricultural production moving. We in Africa should take note of the inability of communist countries to feed their people. And we don't exactly have to listen humbly to Chinese or Russian advice in this matter, or depend wholly on their experience for forming our judgement. Here in Africa we have specifically African experiences of the different types of co-operative farming. In Kenya and Tanganyika, for example, there are flourishing co-operative schemes which are firmly based on the principle of peasant land-ownership. In Ghana, on the other hand, state farms were created on communist lines with shocking results. When Nkrumah was ousted, the statistics he left behind showed that the 105 State Farm Corporations he had created in 1962, and financed by an investment of more than £4 million, had shown losses of almost £2½ million in only two years.

I personally saw the Chinese hunger which was a direct result of the commune experiment. Agricultural 'reform' therefore is a subject which I cannot take lightly. Even Moscow, with its own bitter experience as guide, criticised the heady enthusiasm (on the part of the leaders—not on the part of the peasants!) of Peking's rush into communes. Certainly, the unholy mess China made of that programme gives her no cause to advise us about reorganisation of our peasantry. The regimentation of the Chinese peasants, and the organisation of the countryside in order that it might be better exploited for the benefit of industry, were carried out not for the good of the people but for doctrinaire reasons. The Chinese leaders also saw this policy as a means of gaining greater control over each individual by breaking traditional family ties. What they called the 'feudal, patriarchal family'—similar in many ways to African family groupings— was to be replaced by the 'collective' family of the commune. Leisure hours, such as they were, were devoted to indoctrination sessions, study groups, 'volunteer' labour on big (and miserably ill-planned) water conservancy projects or road-building, and the 'mass' pursuit of communist-style culture in the singing of revolutionary songs or watching home-made and very 'progressive' drama.

But the communes, in fact, brought grievous hardship to the individual and economic disaster to the country, for they caused a breakdown in internal trade, a steep fall in state revenues, and a deterioration in agricultural production. As in the case of many of Russia's collective farms, the inefficiency of the accounting system and the lack of trained personnel to supervise and run vast farming units led to huge mistakes and enormous waste. Worst of all was the utter weariness of the peasants, burdened day in and day out by incessant, backbreaking toil, military drill, long indoctrination sessions, poor food and the deprivation of home comforts. It was all one great, appalling experiment in the dehumanisation of a people.

What with a 'great leap forward' that made the Chinese fall flat on their face, what with people's communes bringing untold hardship to the masses, what with backyard furnaces producing pig-iron that even party organs declared to be fit only for the rubbish heap, China—a land groaning with hunger and over-population—is not yet exactly what you would call an inspiration. For all their air of self-confidence, the Chinese are on very shaky ground when they talk about economic construction and self-reliance. So here again Peking has no alternative but to fall back on revolution as its great message for Africa.

The advice about self-reliance and refusing 'neo-colonialist' aid might be worth listening to if our small, poor, and in many ways ill-equipped countries in Africa were willing to wait one, two or more centuries to lift themselves up by their bootstraps. But we cannot afford to think in terms of centuries; we must think in terms of decades. Most of the world is moving ahead and we want to move with it. If our pace is a bit slower than some, very well—at least we must move. Even as the Queen in *Alice in Wonderland* said, it may take all the running we can do just to stay in the same place. We do not dare to let any aspect of our development deteriorate and we must make every improvement possible.

◘   ◘

Chou En-lai's advice, interpreted in the context of all the relevant facts and of China's own ghastly experience, is an open invitation to backwardness.

Yet the urging of self-reliance, in its purity, is something that should command the attention of all African countries. It is a reproach to those who have not yet awakened to the reality that the building of our countries is our own business and not the business of the foreigner: those who, instead of looking inward and planning to harness their own strength, always look outward to the foreigner's loans. It is a reproach, too, to those who adopt towards foreign aid the irresponsible attitude that there is always more where the last lot came from, and who make this an excuse for waste.

We know now that the politicians lied when they led us to believe that independence was synonymous with luxury and ease. Having learnt the bitter truth that prosperity, luxury and ease depend upon our own sweat and toil, let us then get down to the task of nation-building in the clear awareness that our future lies in our own hands, not in the hands of the foreigner.

EIGHT

Faith in Africa

Yesterday, we followed the road that the colonial master pointed out to us. Today, we are free to go whichever way we choose. Because of the humiliations we suffered as colonial peoples, we tend to reject as unacceptable the political systems the colonialists bequeathed to us. This is understandable—but only up to a point. To reject a system merely because you don't like its proponent is, to say the least, a sign of immaturity. Equally, to swallow wholesale any system whose proponent you happen to like is also a sign of immaturity.

From each ideological hemisphere, Africa can find something good to borrow. With these borrowings, blended with the moral and ethical principles that marked the African way of life before the white men came, we can develop political systems that will serve our particular needs and aspirations.

Who says that Africa—past and present—has nothing to offer the world? The famous Arab traveller, Ibn Batuta, wrote in his account of a visit to the kingdom of Melle (Mali) in 1352-53:

The Negroes are seldom unjust and have a greater horror of
injustice than any other people. Their Sultan shows no mercy
to anyone who is guilty of the least act of it. There is complete
security in their country. Neither traveller nor inhabitant in
it has anything to fear from robbers or men of violence. [1]

What an example for emulation by us of modern Africa! Who
among us would not readily exchange for such peace and just
order all the thugs and rebel gangs, robbers and festering
corruption that now plague so many of our countries? What has
so changed in us that we should spurn the laudable moral
principles of our ancestors?

In the kingdom of Songhai in the nineties of the fifteenth
century, Mohammed Ibn Abubakr el Thure came to the throne.
His first act, the historian C. R. Niven observes, 'was a remark-
able one for those days or for any other'. [2] He reduced the size
of his armies, leaving only a small standing army to cope with
internal troubles. He thought his kingdom needed rest and
recovery. In modern language, you would call this 'disarmament'—just that very thing the world powers have been
searching for in all the cellars of Geneva for years. (I admit
that, as things now are in the world, no modern country would
be likely to survive long after so simple a form of unilateral
disarmament; but this does not entirely pull my case to pieces.)
It would seem that this excellent gesture of Ibn Abubakr has
lost all its appeal for us today, seeing that impecunious Africa
currently spends hundreds of millions of pounds yearly on
armaments and military build-up. Armaments for what? No
amount of arms that independent Africa can now amass will
enable us to withstand any of the significant world powers in
an all-out war. If the arms are not for use against far-away
potential aggressors, they can only be for our closer neighbours
—other Africans. Several African countries have already justified their military build-up by the argument that they need to
counter-balance a neighbouring country's military build-up.

The long and short of it is that we have our own miniature arms race—miniature in comparison with that of the great powers, but hugely burdensome in relation to our slender resources. Arms are being bought with foreign aid that should be more beneficially employed in economic development. Mark you, we think there is nothing paradoxical in lecturing others on the benefits of disarmament!

My great-great-great-grandfather may not have been exactly a cousin (even umpteen times removed) of any of the Pharaohs, but I take pride as an African in the fact that the Europeans first learnt geometry from the Egyptians; and see what they have been able to do with that science since the Pharaohs! Not that we must get overvauntful of Africa's contribution to humanity. We have just cause for pride in many things, but let it be reasoned pride. Measured with small countries like Britain and Greece, Spain and Portugal, Giant Africa's contribution to the totality of human civilisation has so far been very modest. The isolated achievements in our past do not measure up to the vast treasuries of achievement bequeathed to humanity by other peoples.

In this sense, we are a new people. But mankind is capable of receiving from us great new things. Now is Africa's historic moment to make up for our deficiencies of the past. Now is the time to prove in fuller measure than we have so far done that the white and yellow racists are utterly, blindly wrong; that if we are not yet where the leading civilised countries are today, it is not because we cannot get there.

To prove our case, we need peace. And to have peace, we must reject—wholly and decisively—the call by China and any other power to *indiscriminate revolution*. There is no surer way to miss this vital peace than to attach ourselves to the apron-strings of a China that has so clearly marked herself an enemy of peace.

If we must have an example to emulate, let it be a peaceful example; let it be constructive, not destructive. For such a purpose, give me the example of India, which has led the world in recent times in a genuine search for peaceful coexistence; give me Denmark, Sweden and Norway, which for two hundred years have left their neighbours in peace and developed just and democratic societies where collective needs and individual freedom are harmonised; give me, for all her involuted and incomprehensible ways, Britain which has learned to give up imperial power without die-hard and violent resistance to the 'wind of change'.*

China is a nation with an ancient civilisation and a popular culture rich in wise sayings. Few parts of Africa can boast anything comparable with China's civilised past. But Africa too has her rich store of ancient adages. One of these often leaps to my mind when I think of China's relations with Africa and attitude to Africans. It runs: 'The vulture does not qualify to peddle cures for baldness.' With time, Africa will cure her baldness—her economic and other forms of backwardness. But I don't believe that in the China of today we can find the right medicament.

Hate China? No. Hatred wastes energy and time. We need all the energy, time and other resources we can muster to concentrate on the all-important fight against poverty, ignorance and disease, and on the improvement of our people's standard of living.

Don't hate China—but don't trust her either.

Trust ourselves—have faith in Africa.

I have faith in the future of Africa, a faith as strong as only an African heart can hold.

I have faith in an Africa where neither the foreigner's rod nor the dictator's heel shall be felt.

I have faith in an Africa with democracy and justice so firmly entrenched that the common man can laugh with pitying contempt at anyone who says we need a violent revolution to achieve progress.

* But note, I would not have us swallow *everything* from any of these nations!

I have faith in an Africa too sensible to allow nuclear and other armaments to play a part in her internal and external policies.

The road to such a future is no easy road. So much the greater, then, must our efforts be to follow it; and so much greater the prize for our achieving.

I have faith in the future of Africa.

APPENDICES

I

Chou En-lai's Tour of Africa, December 1963 – February 1964

United Arab Republic	December 14–21, 1963
Algeria	December 21–27, 1963
Morocco	December 27–30, 1963
Albanian Interlude	December 31, 1963–January 9, 1964
Tunisia	January 9–10, 1964
Ghana	January 11–15, 1964
Mali	January 16–21, 1964
Guinea	January 21–27, 1964
Sudan	January 28–30, 1964
Ethiopia	January 30–February 1, 1964
Somalia	February 1–4, 1964

The aims of Chou En-lai's African tour, as stated by himself to reporters of the Ghana News Agency on January 15, 1964, were very simple. The purpose, he said, was 'to enhance the mutual understanding between China and friendly African countries, strengthen traditional friendship between the Chinese people and the African people, further develop the relations of friendship and co-operation between China and the African countries, increase our knowledge and learn useful things from the African people.'

But, to judge from the amount of speculation on this subject in the world press, nobody was prepared to believe that China's aims were as simple and innocent as that. Peking's objectives, then and now, can be summarised as follows:

1. *To win friends and allies in the bid to end China's political isolation.* China has no real friend in the Western world and, since the eruption of the Sino-Soviet ideological dispute, most communist countries—with the notable exception of Albania—have aligned themselves with the Soviet Union. Peking will find it easier to win friends in the relatively uncommitted new countries than in either the East or the West.

2. *To repair the damage done to China's image and reputation by her imperialism in Tibet and unprovoked attack on India.* Most African countries had no independent voice at the time when the Chinese People's Liberation Army over-ran Tibet in 1950. They failed in 1962 to take an unequivocal stand on India's behalf over China's aggression. However, they have been deeply disturbed by these naked displays of power. The Chinese would like to show Africans that they are not quite so villainous as they have been portrayed. This view is supported by the uncharacteristically soft line adopted by Chou during most of his African tour.

3. *China is making a bid for the leadership of 'we coloured peoples'* (*Chou's phrase*). Having worsted India and dethroned it as the leading Asian power, China, seeking to isolate the Soviet Union with the argument that the Russians are non-Asians, aims to dominate all future Afro-Asian gatherings. At the time of Chou's tour of Africa, a 'second Bandung' was envisaged by Peking as a forum for condemning both the Western 'imperialists' and the Soviet Union which, by Chinese definition, now belongs to the despicable imperialist species.

Thus, China presents herself to us as a coloured, underdeveloped, anti-imperialist and anti-colonialist country—and therefore 'one of us'. At the same time, we in the underdeveloped world are supposed to realise and accept that, though a member of our 'poor-man's club', China is ahead of us in all respects, including economic development, population and military power. So, clearly, China must lead us—so the Chinese communists say.

4. *To present China as the sole champion of the Third World, and Russia as a betrayer of the cause of the oppressed peoples.* Confronted by grim nuclear reality, the Soviet Union is now more cautious and sophisticated in furthering communism and her own national interests.

She will still encourage revolution where it seems safe for her to do so, but in other cases, she will collaborate with and help movements and governments which are far from revolutionary, if she thinks this will serve her purposes. This China seizes on as proving that the Soviet Union has betrayed the communist revolution, leaving China as its only true upholder. It is in this role that China presents herself as the sole and unrivalled champion of Africa and the developing world, for the Western powers are regarded by the new nations as imperialists, actual or potential.

Of immediate importance to China is the winning of Africa's moral support in the Sino-Soviet dispute. Since most of Africa has shown the desire to steer clear of this cold war in the communist camp, Peking's aim here can only be achieved by a roundabout method, one which will manœuvre China into a position of leadership in the developing world. This achieved, African support—Peking calculates —will follow automatically.

5. *To encourage independent Africa to destroy Western political and economic influence.* 'West' here includes the Soviet Union which, according to China, has turned 'white', 'rich' and 'imperialist'. The help which Britain, the United States and other Western countries and the Soviet Union can give to Africa for its benefit (provided Africans keep firm control of the independence they have won) is denounced as 'neo-colonialism'. Only Chinese help, says China, is truly intended for our good.

6. *To take advantage of Africa's political fluidity.* The aim here is to exploit the situation of unavoidable political restlessness and uncertainty in the continent in order to plant the seeds of 'national liberation' and revolutionary war, so that in the resultant disorder and chaos China can get some juicy pickings.

7. *To seek new trade partners outside the Soviet orbit.* Sino-Soviet trade having been affected by the breach between the two countries, China must go farther afield for markets and raw materials. Africa is a fertile field for both.

8. *To win recognition from more African states and thus increase China's chances of entry into the United Nations and other international bodies.* Because of the standing debate as to which of the two —the communist government on the mainland or the non-communist government in Formosa—is the true representative of the Chinese people, recognition of, and diplomatic relations with, 'China' has been an international game of hide and seek. Some countries, of which Rwanda and the Malagasy Republic have been notable

examples, recognised and established relations with Nationalist China (Formosa) as a demonstration of their fear of, or aversion for, communism. Others, like Guinea and Nkrumah's Ghana, have had relations with Communist China to show their attachment to the socialist camp. Others yet, among which we may count Kenya and Tunisia, have established relations with Red China for the reason that her size, population and influence in world affairs make it unrealistic to ignore her. The Cameroon Republic and a few other countries have either refused to establish relations or have broken them off in protest against Red China's subversion in their countries. A small handful, among which are Nigeria and Malawi, have adopted an ambiguous position by recognising both Chinese governments while maintaining diplomatic relations with none.

Though, as shown above, a pro-Peking policy does not necessarily follow relations with Red China, it is a likely outcome in so far as United Nations membership is concerned, since recognition of Red China almost automatically disputes the position of Nationalist China.

As both Chinese governments adamantly maintain that there is only one and indivisible China, most African countries, who would rather steer clear of this dispute, find themselves in a dilemma during United Nations debates and votes on the China issue. This dilemma is increased by Red China's implacable demand, that Nationalist China should be expelled from the United Nations before her own entry.

II

African Diplomatic Relations with the Two Chinas (as at May 1966)

Note: The dates given are either those of the formal decision of recognition or of the actual establishment of relations. The main source is *Africa Report*, January 1965.

Country	People's Republic of China (Peking)	Republic of China (Taipeh)
Algeria	July 1962	None
Burundi	Jan. 1964; severed early 1965	None
Cameroon	None	Feb. 1960
Central African Republic	Oct. 1964; severed late 1965	June 1962; severed Nov. 1964
Chad	None	Jan. 1962
Congo (Brazzaville)	Feb. 1964	Sept. 1960; severed April 1964
Congo (Kinshasa)	None	Dec. 1961
Dahomey	Nov. 1964; severed Dec. 1965	Jan. 1962; lapsed; re-established May 1966
Ethiopia	Jan. 1964	None
Gabon	None	Dec. 1960

Country	People's Republic of China (Peking)	Republic of China (Taipeh)
Gambia	None	None
Ghana	July 1960; severed late 1966	None
Guinea	Oct. 1959	None
Ivory Coast	None	July 1963
Kenya	Dec. 1963	None
Liberia	None	Aug. 1957
Libya	None	Dec. 1959
Malagasy Republic	None	July 1960
Malawi	None	None
Mali	Oct. 1960	None
Mauritania	July 1965	Nov. 1961
Morocco	Oct. 1958	None
Niger	None	July 1963
Nigeria	None	None
Rwanda	None	July 1962
Senegal	None	June 1960; severed Sept. 1964
Sierra Leone	None	Sept. 1963
Somalia	Dec. 1960	None
Sudan	Dec. 1958	None
Tanzania	Dec. 1961	None
Togo	None	April 1960
Tunisia	Jan. 1964	None
Uganda	Oct. 1962	None
United Arab Republic	May 1956	None
Upper Volta	None	Dec. 1961
Zambia	Early 1965	None

References

1. The 'Five Principles' and Chinese Practice

1. *Leading Events in India–China Relations 1947–1962*, External Publicity Division, Ministry of External Affairs, New Delhi 1962.
2. Ibid.
3. Robert Ford, *Captured in Tibet*, Harrap, London 1958.
4. Sir Basil J. Gould, *The Jewel in the Lotus*, Chatto and Windus, London 1957
5. Ford, op. cit.
6. *Chang Chiang*, Hankow, July 13, 1957; cited in Nadadur Srinivasan, *Inside Present-day China*, Popular Prakashan, Bombay 1963

2. Peking's Theory of War and Peace

1. David Shub, *Lenin*, Doubleday, New York 1948
2. *A Reply to Peking: Soviet Government Statement*, Soviet Booklet No. 122, London, September 1963
3. Cited in "The Differences Between Comrade Togliatti and Us", *People's Daily*, Peking, December 31, 1962
4. *A Reply to Peking* . . . , op. cit.
5. Ibid.
6. Ibid.
7. "The Leaders of the CPSU are the Greatest Splitters of Our Time", *People's Daily*, Peking, February 4, 1964.

3. Permanent Revolution

1. *Washington Post*, January 12, 1964
2. Shub, op. cit.

4. THE SECOND SCRAMBLE FOR AFRICA

1. *Peking Review*, No. 3, 1964
2. W. A. C. Adie, "Chinese Policy Towards Africa", in Sven Hamrell and Carl Widstrand, *The Soviet Bloc, China and Africa*, Pall Mall, London 1965, p. 43
3. *Daily Nation*, Nairobi, February 4, 1963
4. *Sunday Times*, Cape Town, September 8, 1963
5. *China Mail*, Hong Kong, July 6, 1964
6. *East African Standard*, October 28, 1965

5. REVOLUTIONARY SITUATIONS: I

1. Shub, op. cit.

6. REVOLUTIONARY SITUATIONS: II

1. Suzanne Labin, *Les Colonialistes Chinois en Afrique*, China Publishing Co., Taipeh, Taiwan, n.d.
2. *Peking Review*, No. 12, 1964
3. *Indian Observer*, January 31, 1964
4. Cf. "Operazione Mambo Verde", *Vita*, Rome, June 1966

7. INVITATION TO BACKWARDNESS

1. *U.S. News and World Report*, May 27, 1963
2. Cf. *East African Standard*, February 3, 1964
3. *Drum*, Lagos, August 1964
4. These figures are drawn from a programme, "On the Short Memory of Certain Theoreticians", broadcast over the European service of Radio Moscow on August 31, 1963
5. A. Doak Barnett, *Communist Economic Strategy: The Rise of Mainland China*, National Planning Association, Washington, D.C. 1959

8. FAITH IN AFRICA

1. Cited in C. R. Niven, *A Short History of Nigeria*, Longmans, London 1948
2. Ibid.

Index

11/1/67

53024

DT
38.9
C5
H4

HEVI, EMMANUEL
    THE DRAGON'S EMBRACE.

DATE DUE

FEB 1 9 2016	

Fernald Library
Colby-Sawyer College
New London, New Hampshire

GAYLORD   PRINTED IN U.S.A.